BREAK
THROUGH
**a leader's
greatest lesson**

BREAK
THROUGH
a leader's
greatest lesson

Dr. Paul Homoly, CSP

First printing 2007
Second printing 2008
Third printing 2008

ISBN 978-0-9776289-1-9

Cover design by Athena Marketing and text design by Breiding Marketing, LLC.

ATTENTION CORPORATIONS, UNIVERSITIES, COLLEGES AND PROFESSIONAL ORGANIZATIONS: Quantity discounts are available on bulk purchases of this book. Excerpts can also be created to fit specific needs. For information, please contact Homoly Communications Institute, 2125 Southend Drive, Suite 250, Charlotte, NC 28203, (800) 294-9370, www.paulhomoly.com.

Dedication

To the students of my leadership workshops, who, by allowing me to make you better leaders, have made me a better coach.

Contents

Acknowledgment

I remember getting this very cool model airplane for my birthday from my uncle Frank when I was a little boy. My mom told me to write a thank-you letter, but I got so busy gluing the airplane together, I forgot to write the letter.

Writing this book has been like building that airplane. I'm not going to make the same mistake twice and not write a thank-you letter to all the people who helped me glue it together.

Deserving special recognition is Patty Blackburn, my neighbor, golfing buddy, and all-too-often wine-drinking accomplice. Her influence is evident on every page. Patty's interest, insight and encouragement have helped this project take flight.

A big thank you goes to my team in Charlotte, North Carolina: Janet Plantier, Joan Cianciolo and Julie Potter. They are the people who keep the assembly line of my business running and hold all the pieces together.

Liz Snyder, my instructional designer, who, throughout this project has been an incredible sounding board, advisor and contributor. Liz was there when the project first lifted off, and she's been an amazing co-pilot.

A special thank you goes to my fiancée, Lisa Stimmer, for creating that special place in my heart where I can go and feel love. She refuels my engine and helps me soar.

And a big high-five to my graphic design team of Tim Breiding and Nikki Harrison (Breiding Marketing), Nancy Lashley (Athena Marketing) and Judy Cole for streamlining this project and making it look great.

Chapter One
Dan

For the first time in his life, Dan Morgan was scared. His job and his life had been pretty good up to now. He did okay in undergrad, despite the keggers. Grad school went better. He settled down and surprised himself and most of his buddies when he was recruited by the top companies. Soon after graduation, Dan fell in love with Diane, who had a smile he could feel from across the room. Things really came together for Dan after he and Diane were married.

Dan landed at Granite Financial Services, one of the top financial services companies located in the heart of the business district in downtown Chicago. With a promising career in hand, he and Diane began fulfilling their dream of a family. A new job, a new baby daughter, a new marriage – all of it rocked Dan's world. For the first time in his life he had people – many people, important people – looking to him to make the right decisions and do the right things. It was time for him to make his move.

And by focusing on what he knew best, move he did. Dan worked long and hard, making amazing things happen. His rising star shot through the organization, surpassing everyone's expectations. From his start in sales, where he doubled his quota and attracted a legion of new clients, he was given bigger and bigger opportunities over the next decade. The more he took on, the more he won. Dan had been bulletproof – until now.

Dan's success came with an unintended consequence – the more he succeeded, the more he advanced. His drift into leadership won him a prize he wasn't ready for.

The promotions seemed fine at first – more money, better perks, more dazzle. Over time, however, Dan slowly started to lose his edge. He no longer had direct client contact, where he could work the magic of his brilliance and the twinkle in his eye. More and more, Dan had to rely on his people to make his magic work, and it wasn't working like it once had.

At first, the declining sales didn't concern him, nor did the fact that a few of his seasoned people quit. A bump in the road, he thought. Soon, though, the sustained tumble of his numbers, combined with the loss of a few more long-term good producers, began to keep Dan awake at night. For the first time, he felt like he was losing and he didn't know how to fix it. Years ago, when it was just Dan and his clients, he could fix anything by working longer and harder. Since losing direct client contact, Dan felt as if he was working with mechanical hands – like those at an arcade. He was losing his grip – on his clients, on his people, and, worst of all, on his confidence.

Chapter Two
Julie

Dan arrived at his office every day at 8 A.M. sharp just as he'd done for the two years since he'd been named CEO. You couldn't see in Dan's eyes that he was worried. He still radiated the same confidence and energy as when he'd first hoisted his champagne glass during the toast welcoming him to the big office in the corner. In his mind though, Dan knew if the numbers kept slipping and people kept leaving, the party would be over.

Dan had no reason to think this day wouldn't be like any other day. He tucked his black Infiniti into his reserved spot in the underground parking deck. He made his way past the security cameras and up the elevator to the top floor, where he was greeted by his assistant Julie McIntyre, whose alert eyes and gray streak in her hair signaled her experience and quiet efficiency.

"Good morning, Dan. Hope this weekend recharged your batteries," Julie said, smiling.

Dan smiled back. "It did Julie. I love springtime."

Julie had become Dan's barometer; she knew the people and the buzz. Julie had been with Granite Financial Services for seven years, working as an administrative assistant for the CEO prior to the CEO Dan had replaced. Julie left to raise her children for several years, then returned, stronger than ever, just in time to help Dan take on the world. After only a few weeks of working with her, he realized she was stronger and smarter than many of the execs on his floor – plus, he loved her smile and sharp wit.

After settling into his office and checking a few e-mails, Dan called Julie in.

"Julie, last week when I addressed the team about our sales numbers and goals, how would you characterize their response?" he asked.

Dan knew he had caught Julie off guard with his question. He rarely asked her opinion of his performance.

Julie glanced at her shoes and said, "I think they got the message. Time will tell what they do with it."

Julie's response was not what Dan had been hoping for. He could tell she was hedging – not telling him what she really thought. And she was not the only one; his marketing director, his head of operations … it seemed like so many people on his team were holding their cards close to their vests. Julie, though, was the last straw. If he couldn't get a straight answer from her, something was really rotten.

"Julie, why is it I feel you're not saying everything that's on your mind?" Dan pressed.

Julie smiled, put her folders on Dan's desk, and sat down across from him. She took a moment, and then began.

"Dan, we've been together now for two years. You're smarter than anyone I've worked with here," she said. "You understand the business, the market, the technology and the competition. What you *don't* understand is how to get your team to respond to your leadership. Your ideas are great, but you're not getting through to people. It's hard to put my finger on it, but I'd say, it seems you're talking *at* people and not *to* them. It's not like you're degrading anyone; you're appropriate in your approach but you're not talking to them in a way they can feel what you're saying. If they can't feel it, they won't remember it, or be compelled to act on it."

Julie's response seemed like a stab from the past. It was not the first time he'd heard this. Dan knew he was not the warm, fuzzy type. Several times when he was evaluated in the 360-degree assessments, his raters scored him low on connecting with them. Dan never worried too much about these low team ratings because his clients loved him, and that, he thought, was what brought home the bacon.

Julie sat motionless and silent as Dan processed his thoughts. Finally, Dan asked, "So, Julie, if you feel I'm not getting through to the team, what do you recommend I do?"

Upon hearing this, Julie knew she had struck a nerve. She had never seen Dan make himself vulnerable. Asking for help showed a new side of him. She liked it, so she decided to take a risk and tell Dan what she had wanted to say for so many months.

Chapter Three
Stanley

Julie began, "Dan, 10 years ago our company enjoyed the highest profitability in our industry sector. In fact, we were almost 30 percent higher than our closest competitors. Topping that off, we had less than one percent employee turnover. People were diving into their work like they couldn't get enough of it."

Dan responded, "Yeah, I know about that time. You guys really made it look easy. Times have changed. We live in a different world now."

"You're right, Dan, we do. However, there's one thing that hasn't changed – the team needs the right kind of leadership to *compel* them to act on the vision. You, Dan, do not *compel* people to act, you *tell* them to act. There's a huge difference."

Dan shifted in his chair.

Julie continued. "During that era of historic profits, this company was led by Stanley Robbins. I worked with him for many years, and I know Stanley made this company magic. Dan, you asked me for a recommendation and here it is: Learn how Stanley moved people to action. Learn how Stanley talked to people and helped them love their work."

Dan had not expected this. He was hoping for some technical or operational fix – something he was good at. Hearing what his company needed, knowing this was his weakness, made Dan exhale hard and look at the ceiling.

After a moment he asked, "What happened to Stanley? I heard he left right at the peak of earnings."

"He did," said Julie. "Some say he got sick, others say he got into some disagreements with the board. After he left, the culture around here changed. Talking about Stanley was not part of the program anymore."

As Dan was about to ask another question, Julie stood and reminded him of his 9:30 A.M. appointment, and offered to continue the conversation later. Julie left Dan's office, and for the rest of the day, Dan's schedule was full and fast.

Staying busy took Dan's mind off his morning talk with Julie, which suited him fine. The idea of being mentored had never appealed to Dan. He liked being his own guy. Somehow, asking for help diminished his idea of what leaders do. He'd gotten this far without a lot of hand holding. Besides, working with an ex-CEO who had quit – or had been fired – didn't seem like good business. By the end of the day, Dan's morning conversation about Stanley shifted to the back burner. He had bigger fish to fry, and working on his communication style to fix his company seemed like firing BBs at an iceberg.

It was late when Dan left his office. Only the cleaning people remained as he punched the elevator button for the parking garage. The day had left his mind numb and he was tired. The elevator door chime at the bottom floor woke him from his stupor and he walked toward his car. It felt good to be going home.

As he opened his car door, he suddenly smelled smoke. He turned around and saw a tall man leaning against a pillar, smoking a cigarette. The man smiled, dropped the cigarette on the concrete and ground it out with his shoe.

"This is a nonsmoking building," Dan reprimanded him. "You shouldn't be smoking."

"From what I hear about how you're running this company, I'm surprised *you're* not smoking," replied the stranger.

Dan was too tired and not in the mood to deal with who-knows-what in the basement parking garage at night. He got into his car and backed out of his space. Dan could see the tall stranger better now in the headlights. He was well dressed in a short-waisted leather jacket, lavender shirt, black slacks, nice shoes. Dan was a bit of a clothes hound himself. The man smiled again and approached Dan's car with a confident stride. He motioned for Dan to open his window. Dan felt safe doing it.

"Can I help you?" asked Dan.

"I think I should be the one asking you that," said the stranger.

"Who are you?"

"I'm Stanley Robbins. You got time for a cup of coffee?"

Chapter Four
A Simple Decision

The ride to a coffee shop in Lincoln Park went quickly. Stanley jumped into Dan's car, and before he knew it, Stanley was giving directions. Dan wasn't worried about Stanley, every security camera had recorded their meeting. Besides, Stanley had a way about him that was interesting, even at the end of a hard day.

During the ride, Dan quizzed Stanley about his exit from Granite Financial. Stanley acknowledged Dan's questions, but said he'd answer them after he got to know Dan a little better.

The coffee shop was the type of place only a regular could find. After Dan and Stanley were seated, Stanley smiled and said, "We have a mutual friend who mentioned you might be interested in meeting."

"It's Julie, isn't it?" asked Dan.

Stanley's knowing smile was nearly answer enough.

"It is. She called me this afternoon and filled me in on a few things."

Stanley talked several minutes about Julie – her history as his personal assistant and friend for years, her incredible loyalty to the company and to him, battles they had won and lost together.

As Stanley spoke, Dan measured him. The more Stanley talked, the more Dan liked what he saw and heard. Stanley looked good. He had thick salt-and-pepper hair, deep smile lines around his eyes – no doubt due to decades of good cheer – and a prosperous and joyful manner Dan could feel from across the table. By Dan's calculations, Stanley must have been in his late seventies, yet the man who was in front of him now had the energy and glow of a college quarterback after winning the homecoming game. It didn't take Dan long to realize the wisdom of Julie's recommendation.

He thought, *If I could bottle up just half of this guy's dazzle and dump it on my team …*

Dan's daydream was interrupted when Stanley said, "Dan, I'll get right to the point. Julie told me you need help getting through to your team. She gave me a pretty good description of what was going on. She knows I can help you. What I need to know is, do you want the help?"

No wasted words here, Dan thought. *It's a simple decision, my favorite kind.*

When Dan answered, he surprised himself. "Stanley, I've known you for less than a half hour, and yet within that time, you invited yourself into my car, convinced me to drive us here, and told me more about Julie in five minutes than I've learned after working with her for two years. If you're saying you can teach me to impact my team the way you've impacted me, I'm in!"

"Good decision," said Stanley. "Julie said you were smart. Now, let's put those brains of yours to good use."

Chapter Five
Leadership and Break Through

Dan got up from the table, walked outside and called Diane to tell her he'd be late. When he returned, he found Stanley walking back from the counter with two more coffees.

"So, what are we going to talk about?" asked Dan as the two men settled back into their seats.

"Two things," said Stanley. "The first is about leadership. The second is how to speak to get your leadership message to break through."

Stanley's tone and energy shoved out any daydream in Dan's head.

"Leadership," Stanley began, "is your ability to create an environment where it's easy for people to succeed and feel better about themselves. You'll hear a lot more complicated definitions, but I've found that the further I got from focusing on this definition, the more hot water I got into.

"There are two parts to my understanding of leadership; the first part is about making it easy for people to succeed. This means giving your people the tools and the processes for success. I understand from Julie that you're doing a great job with that. People also need the right emotional environment. For you, Dan, this is going to be the uphill climb. Like it or not, a big part of a leader's job is to resonate the right vibes to help people be their best. Have you read any of the contemporary leadership books? In *Primal Leadership,* Goleman nails it when he talks about how the leader must set the emotional climate. You set the right emotional climate through how you speak with people. There's no escaping this: how well you speak determines how well you lead. When you set the right climate through your language, you make it easy for people to be their best. That's part of how you can make it easy for people to succeed."

As Stanley spoke, Dan sipped his coffee, but soon into Stanley's lesson, it became obvious to Dan that he'd better take a few notes. He had heard parts of what he was hearing before, but the way Stanley spoke drew him in. Dan grabbed a few napkins and started making notes. What was interesting to Dan was that the moment he started writing, Stanley stopped speaking and waited for him to finish. It seemed it was more important for Dan to learn than it was for Stanley to teach – an important lesson within the lesson.

"The second part of leadership is helping people feel better about themselves," Stanley continued. "There's a lot out there now on customer service and how to create the 'WOW' experience. You read about Nordstrom's, Ritz-Carlton, Disney, and all that's fine, but I'll tell you the best experience anyone can have is a strong positive experience of themselves. When people come away from an encounter feeling better about themselves, it's like getting money from home."

"I had a high school teacher in senior honors English," Stanley went on. "His name was Mr. Kampka. I was an auto shop major, and I'd walk into English class smelling like gasoline – which was a bit of a turnoff with the girls – but I made up for it by being funny. Anyway, Mr. Kampka was magic with me. I loved to write and he knew it. When he'd review my essays, he did it in such a way that brought out *my* best, not *his* best. You see, a good teacher gets the student to feel good about the teacher, but a great teacher gets the students to feel good about themselves. Same is true with leadership. The great leaders get their people to feel good about themselves. When someone has the ability to make you feel better about yourself, you'll never forget them."

Dan was now a step ahead of Stanley as thoughts of his daughter Cassie jumped into his head. He thought, *A good parent gets the child to feel good about the parent, but it's the great parent who gets the child to feel good about themselves – hmmmmm.*

Stanley sensed Dan's mind was wandering.

"Dan, tell me what you're thinking," Stanley said.

"Oh, a couple of things," said Dan. "I couldn't help but think leadership applies to parenting. I'm having a bit of a contest with my teenage daughter, and I may rethink how I'm approaching her."

"Teenagers!" Stanley laughed. "Now you know why alligators eat their young."

"Do you have any kids?" asked Dan.

"I do, a daughter. She's all grown up, happily married, and off my payroll." Stanley replied.

Humor was like the fragrance of Stanley's aftershave – it followed him everywhere, and it seemed like he could make Dan smile anytime he wanted to. *A nice gift to have*, thought Dan. He could have used it a hundred times in the last week.

"You're a funny guy," said Dan. "Are you going to teach me to be funny?"

"I will, but not tonight," Stanley told Dan. "The main thing tonight is this: Everything we talk about from now on will go back to this understanding – leadership is your ability to create an environment in which it's easy for people to succeed and feel better about themselves. Most of this is accomplished through how you speak to people. As a leader, you must speak in a way that aligns listeners to your vision and compels them to take action."

"Do you ever wonder whether you're breaking through to people?" asked Stanley.

"Every day," said Dan. "I worry about that more than anything. I can say the right things, but if it isn't breaking through and not sticking, it's like I never said it. I know they hear me, they can tell me what I said when I ask them, but doing it seems to be another thing."

"Breakthrough is the second thing we're going to talk about tonight," said Stanley. "If you can't break through, you can't lead. How many times in our lives have we been let down by a leader? It might have been a parent, a teacher, a clergyman, a boss, or a friend who had an important message for us, but we didn't get it because the leader didn't break through the clutter in our heads. Their message wasn't prepared well, or they had a slouchy speaking style, or they put no passion in their voice. They may have had great content, but they made their message easy to miss because of their dull style.

"Think about the passages of your life when you needed a leader to break through – growing up, your college years, starting your business, being a parent. Too often, the advice we need just doesn't break through."

"There must be a hundred times when that's happened to me," Dan said. "There was this time in high school when … "

Stanley interrupted and said, "Now, before you start confessing other leaders' sins, let me ask you, how many times have you been the leader who didn't break through?"

Dan smiled. Stanley had hit the nail on the head. "I guess it's happening to me now. I'm saying the right things to my team, but it's not breaking through."

"Dan, your team and everyone else you intend to influence need what all people need from their leaders: to break through with the right words at the right time. Breaking through is when your listeners understand your words and *feel* them. Leaders typically focus on people understanding their words. That's not enough. People have to *feel* your words to be compelled to act.

"Right after I went to work at Granite, I took a trip to Asheville, North

Carolina. I was driving on the Blue Ridge Parkway, top down, in a rented convertible Mustang. It was an overcast day and I was snaking through a valley alongside a stream. I crossed over the stream and the road began to rise. I put my foot into it and surged up the steep incline. Moments later, I was in the overcast, seeing just far enough ahead to stay on the road. Then within a few heartbeats, I broke out of the overcast into the clear – a perfect Carolina blue sky, with sunshine that warmed me to my bones.

"Breaking out of the overcast let me see and feel the sunshine. Dan, when you lead, put your listeners in the passenger seat and let them see and feel the sunshine in your words. That's what breakthrough is."

"It's important to make a distinction between teaching and leading," Stanley continued. "The test of whether you taught something is if the listener can pass a test on it; they can recall what you said. Doing it is another matter. The world is filled with brilliant people who can pass tests, but are broke. The test of leadership is action. No action means you didn't lead. Breaking through means compelling your listeners to take action aligned with your vision."

"Is that what you're going to teach me?" asked Dan.

"No, I'm going to *lead* you," replied Stanley.

Chapter Six
The Leader Speaker

The next few weeks for Dan were jammed – meetings, travel, hassles, and a few little victories. Stanley's advice about helping people feel good about themselves made Dan rethink how he was talking to people, and it seemed to be working. Nothing major, he just noticed a bit of the edge was out of some of his relationships, or maybe the edge was out of him, and people were responding differently. Either way, things seemed better.

One day, Julie and Dan were walking back from a meeting a few blocks from their office.

"Have you to talked to Stanley again?" Julie asked.

"Not yet," said Dan. "He's an interesting guy, though he doesn't open up too much about himself."

"Stanley's like that," said Julie. "Until he knows someone, he keeps his boundaries up. He called me a few days ago and put himself on your schedule. You know the late afternoon meeting you have today with the tax department? It's really with Stanley."

Dan looked at Julie, who had an expression on her face like she had just gotten away with something.

"Sounds like you two are joined at the hip on this thing," said Dan.

Julie smiled. "Stanley said for you to bring some paper this time. He said writing notes on napkins is not leader-like."

Later that afternoon, Dan left work and walked a few blocks to Fox and Obel food market grocery on East Illinois Street for his meeting with Stanley. He found him wandering around in the wine section, rubbing his chin, trying to read the labels.

"Drinking already? It's not even five o'clock yet," ribbed Dan.

Stanley smiled. "I'm not a big drinker. It doesn't do that much for me. A lot of people drink to get loose. I was born loose. It's like they say, 'If you're already in Detroit, you don't need a bus to get there.'"

After Stanley bought four bottles of wine, he and Dan found a corner table and settled in, Dan drinking a tall latté and Stanley drinking cream soda.

"If you don't drink, why did you just buy over $300 worth of wine?" asked Dan.

Stanley winked. "It's just in case I get company. You know, Dan, you can never tell what kind of wine a woman likes. Just when you have her pegged as a chardonnay lover, she wants a stout cabernet."

"So, it sounds like you're not married," said Dan.

"I used to be, many years ago. In fact, I've been married twice. My first wife was the love of my life. She died and left this big hole in my life. My second wife turned out to be the devil, but she had great legs," said Stanley.

"Wine and women are easy to appreciate, but tough to figure out," Stanley continued. "A leader's speaking style is easy to figure out."

Wine is too complicated. Leaders, when they speak – I call them 'leader speakers' – are not. As far as I'm concerned, you can put most leader speakers into four categories based on two things: how much they know and how well they express themselves. Did you bring some paper?"

Dan pulled out a few folded sheets of yellow paper from his jacket and clicked his pen into gear.

Stanley took Dan's paper and drew a square, then divided it into four quadrants. He labeled the vertical portion of the square, "Content Expertise" the horizontal, he labeled "Expressive Range." He then wrote "Narrator," "Professor," "Entertainer" and "Leader" in the four quadrants.

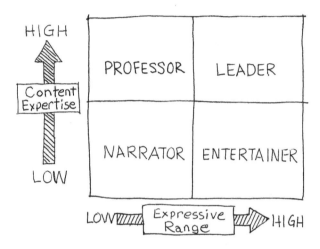

"Like I was saying, when it comes to leader speakers, there are four types. You've got those who are novices and can't express themselves. I call them *narrators* – minimal expertise and narrow expressive range. How they got to be leaders, I'll never understand.

"Then there are the content experts – absolute know-it-alls who don't express themselves well. Those I call the *professors* – content experts with narrow expressive range. They know their stuff, but it's a death march listening to them.

"The third category of leader speakers are those who have minimal content expertise, but have a broad, commanding and expressive range. They tell stories and use humor. People love to listen to them. I call them the *entertainers*. There's not a lot of meat to their talks, but they're fun to listen to.

"The last category is the *leader speaker* who has significant content expertise, *and* broad expressive range. I call them *leaders* – they know what they're talking about and listening to them feels like a gift."

As Stanley spoke, Dan was thinking about all the leader speakers he'd heard. He was most curious about where he fit in, but before Dan could start analyzing himself, Stanley asked, "Who do you know that fits into one of these categories?"

Dan jumped right in. "My first boss after I graduated was a professor all the way. He knew more stuff, but it felt like a beating listening to him."

"Think back to the other day," said Stanley. "What did I say was a good definition of leadership?"

Dan shot back, "Leadership is the ability to create an environment where it's easy for people to succeed and feel better about themselves."

"How did your old boss fit that criteria based on how he spoke?" asked Stanley.

"He didn't, and when I think about it in terms of how you define leadership, instead of feeling better about ourselves, his speaking style made us afraid of him. He knew so much more than we rookies knew, we lived with constant deficits," replied Dan.

"It's interesting you say he contributed to your fears. Fear is another distinguishing factor among leader speakers," said Stanley.

Stanley added more to his diagram, writing in the words "Focus" and "Fear" in each of the quadrants.

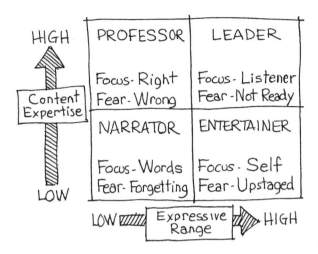

"Each of the four types of leader speakers has a focus," Stanley began. "The narrator focuses on the words. He reads his talks from notes or projected slides. That's where he gets his label. He's not speaking, he's narrating his visual aids or his notes. His focus is making sure he doesn't leave anything out and that all his words are right. Because his focus is on his words, his greatest fear is forgetting the words. His focus *creates* his fear. To combat his fear of forgetting, he memorizes as much as he can. And in the instant he memorizes his words, he has more to forget, which adds more fear, which he combats with more memorization, and the focus/fear cycle creates paralysis and huge levels of anxiety. One big source of leader speaker anxiety comes from overmemorization. The best way to guarantee you'll never forget what you're going to say is to not memorize it.

"The focus of the professor is on being right," Stanley continued. "After all, professors have invested a huge effort in learning all the ropes, and they often see their role as one who knows all the answers. If the professors' focus is on being right, what do you think their greatest source of fear is?"

"Being wrong," said Dan.

"You bet," said Stanley. "And to combat being wrong, professors add more and more data to their talks to strengthen their position. The more they add, the more potential there is for being wrong, so they add more stuff, and on and on. It's almost impossible for a professor leader to give a 20-minute talk worth listening to because professor leaders are convinced they need at least an hour to pile up their bull and smother listeners with the details."

"That sounds exactly like my first boss," said Dan.

"The focus of the entertainer leader speaker is on themselves," said Stanley. "The entertainers are very concerned about what others think of them. In many ways, they're like the stand-up comedian who is at the center of attention with a spotlight on them. The greatest fear of the entertainers is that someone else is more entertaining, or is the center of everyone's attention. If the entertainer's focus is being the center of attention, what do you think their greatest fear is?"

"That someone else gets the listeners' attention," said Dan.

"Yes, and to combat the fear, what does the entertainer do?" asked Stanley.

"Try to become more entertaining by demanding more attention?"

"Right on," said Stanley. "Entertainer leader speakers don't share the limelight. Understand, entertainers are great to listen to, but their self-centeredness doesn't make it easy for others to grow, and listeners certainly don't come away feeling better about themselves."

Stanley got Dan thinking about how he'd been guilty of many of the sins Stanley had described.

"The last category of leader speakers I call leaders," said Stanley. "Leaders have command of the content *and* a broad expressive range, but just because they have a broad range doesn't mean they always have to use it. They can hold back on expressiveness – stories, metaphors, humor – and present as professors when it serves the listener and situation, or they can present as entertainers when the occasion calls for it.

"The leader category is the only one where the focus is on the listener. This focus creates an environment where it's easier for listeners to succeed and feel better about themselves. The greatest fear of the leader is that the listener is not ready to grow or act. One role of the leader speaker is to help listeners become ready for mission-critical initiatives."

"I know," said Dan. "I spend too much of my time getting people up to speed."

"Leaders are often in an expert/novice relationship with the people they're leading," Stanley said. "You're the expert on the topic and you're talking to people who have less expertise or experience about the topic. There's an expert/novice relationship between doctors and their patients, financial advisors and their clients, auto mechanics and their customers, parents and their children. When there's an expert/novice relationship, there's what I call a knowledge gap."

Stanley drew an illustration on Dan's notes.

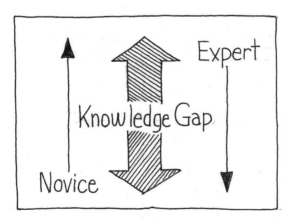

"To get people to grow, or as you put it, get them up to speed, you need to close the knowledge gap.

"As a leader, you have choices about how to do that. You can drag them up to your level or you can go to theirs, then nudge them up to the level they need to be to act with confidence. Typically, leaders try to educate novices and close the gap by bringing the novices to their level."

Dan jumped in. "I've got a great example of that. Last year, I went to my dentist and her hygienist got a hold of me and gave me a 20-minute lecture on the perils of gum disease, using all the dental terms she'd ever learned. I still have no idea what she was talking about."

"And I bet you still don't floss, do you?" asked Stanley.

Dan laughed.

Stanley said, "That's a great example of attempting to drag a novice up to the level of an expert. It takes a lot of energy on the part of the expert, and often frustrates and confuses the novice. It certainly doesn't make it easy for the novice to succeed or feel better about themselves. A more leader-like way of closing the knowledge gap is for the expert to go to the level of the novice, then nudge them up to the level of understanding they need to achieve to act with confidence."

"You mean 'dumbing it down' so people get it?" Dan asked.

"Don't come at it from the perspective of dumbing it down," warned Stanley. "That attitude will take away from your energy. Think of it as seeing it through their eyes. The focus here is on understanding what they know, as opposed to educating them to what they don't know. Look back at the quadrants of leader speakers. The professor speaker will attempt to lead by bringing people to his level by educating them. The leader speaker will lead by understanding his people. He'll understand what their vision is, then start there. The smart leader knows you can't get people to see further than their vision. Learn what your followers' vision is, then through this process of breakthrough I'm teaching you, get them to better see *your* vision. Close the knowledge gap by going to them first, then nudge them up to your level. Breakthrough does that."

Stanley slid the drawing in front of Dan and told him to put an "X" in the quadrant that best described his leader speaker style. By now, it was very clear to Dan that he was a professor – a lot of content, not a lot of listener focus. Stanley then asked Dan to put a star in the quadrant where he wanted to be. Dan immediately put his star in the leader quadrant, thinking the answer to Stanley's question was too obvious.

Stanley drew an arrow going from professor to leader.

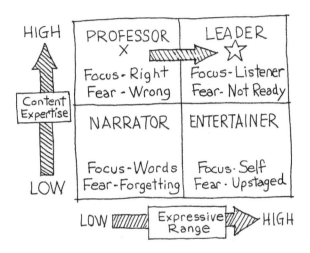

"Dan, if you want to be a better leader speaker, what direction must your speaking style develop in – more content expertise or more expressive range?" asked Stanley.

"More expressive range," answered Dan.

"What does that tell you about how to prepare your talks?" asked Stanley.

"It tells me I need to prepare my delivery more and worry less about the content," said Dan. Never had he considered working on his delivery to become a better leader. This did not feel right to Dan.

"You're saying I need to be more animated, tell stories and use humor to be a better leader. To tell you the truth, that isn't me," said Dan.

Stanley paused for a moment, then said, "Follow me." He hopped up, grabbed his grocery bag full of wine, and headed to the back of the store, with Dan right behind. Just before they got to the produce section, Stanley stopped.

"You see those tall beer coolers back there?" Stanley said. "Walk over to them and then return. When you get back I want you to tell me what you noticed."

Dan smiled and did as Stanley asked. He walked past the produce, the soft drinks and the snacks. He got to the coolers and returned.

"What did you notice?" asked Stanley.

"Nothing much. Looks like a normal store to me."

"Nothing caught your eye?"

"Other than that red onion, nothing," said Dan.

"Tell me about the onion."

"There's a red onion in the middle of the pile of yellow ones."

"Show it to me," said Stanley.

Dan returned to the onions. Stanley followed.

"Here it is," said Dan. "It's a red onion in the middle of all the yellow ones and someone stuck chili peppers around the stem."

"Why did this get your attention?" Stanley asked.

"It stood out from the rest and with the chili peppers you couldn't miss it. I bet ... "

Dan stopped in midsentence, and smiled at Stanley.

"You did this, didn't you?" Dan asked.

Stanley nodded. "If you want to be noticed, you have to stand out from the rest of the pack, otherwise you're just another onion. If you want people to hear you, you must sound different. Too many people in leadership roles all sound the same. Start expanding your expressive range. Tell some stories, have some fun, put a few chili peppers into your talks, and you'll begin to break through."

Dan was amused, but not convinced. He shook his head. "Stories, fun, chili peppers – it really isn't me at all. Besides, I'm afraid it will interfere with my credibility," said Dan.

"No one has ever lost credibility by being interesting," smiled Stanley.

"That may be true," said Dan, "but it's still hard to swallow."

Stanley reached in his grocery bag and handed Dan a bottle of pinot noir and said, "Wash it down with this."

Chapter Seven
Earning Attention

As Dan drove home, he played back his meeting with Stanley. From what he could tell, Stanley was living large. He looked great in his golf shirt, had excellent taste in wine, and, to top it off, he was dating! As he and Stanley left the grocery store, Stanley suggested that Dan become more aware of people on his team and their speaker styles. The conversation about the leader speaker types, and discovering he needed to expand his expressive range to be more effective, haunted him a bit. Plus, he wasn't sure how to do it. Interestingly, though Dan didn't feel great about it, he decided he was going to try.

Dan thought, *What was it about Stanley that influenced me?*

There were subtle things about Stanley he hadn't seen in many people. Stanley's ideas were solid, but more than that, he had a contagious liveliness and it was easy to feel Stanley's words.

By the time Dan pulled into his driveway, he had figured it out and laughed as he thought, *He's making it easy for me to succeed.*

The following week went quickly. Dan began to notice speaking styles. Allen in taxes was a professor all the way, so was Bonnie in human resources. In fact, most people on his team were professors, which made him wonder if that wasn't contributing to his company's problems.

One day he mentioned it to Julie. "Have you noticed there are not a lot of expressive people around here?" he asked.

Julie laughed. "No kidding. You're beginning to sound like Stanley. I remember him saying one of the biggest problems highly educated professionals have is expressing themselves in a way that's interesting. Do you find Stanley an interesting speaker?"

"Absolutely," said Dan. "It's hard not to listen to him."

"Did you know he has a Ph.D. in organizational development, as well as an MBA, *and* he's a CPA?"

"No, I didn't."

"Stanley can go toe-to-toe in a technical conversation with just about anyone in the financial services industry about tax issues, investment allocation practices, world economic theory. You name it, he knows the landscape, but unlike all the technical financial wizards, Stanley can connect with just about anyone on their level. That's why Stanley is a great leader. Hang in there with Stanley, Dan, he won't let you down."

"You have a lot of faith in him, don't you?" asked Dan.

"I do," said Julie. "For lots of reasons."

Dan and Stanley's next meeting was over drinks at The Chicago Chop House, a quintessential Chicagoland restaurant. Dan was drinking Jack Daniels and ginger ale, and Stanley was drinking a Corona with lime. After they clicked glasses and toasted to more warm, sunny days in Chicago, Stanley said, "Dan, the currency of great leader speaking is earning, then holding, your listeners' attention. The phrase, 'Can I have your attention, please?' doesn't work. The people you lead don't *give* you their attention, you must *earn* it. There's too much going on in people's heads for them just to shut it off and listen to you. Very few leaders understand this. They think their position is enough to earn and hold attention. It isn't.

"One of the best books I've read on speaking is called *Presentations Plus* by David Peoples. In it, he has a diagram that makes a lot of sense."

Dan whipped out his notepaper and pen and Stanley drew a simple chart.

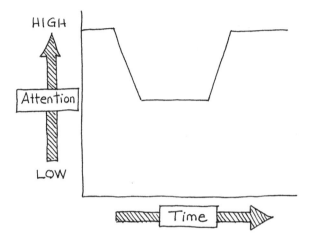

"Typically, you have a listener's attention in the beginning of your talk and at the end," explained Stanley. "In the beginning, they're listening, but after a short time, a few seconds, they begin to drift and lose focus on what you're saying and start paying attention to their own issues – their family, personal problems, their sick cat. People can think a lot faster than you can talk, so they get a hundred thoughts in edgewise while you're talking. At the end of your talk when you say, 'So in conclusion' they perk up again because they know it's time to go to the restroom, check their e-mails or go eat."

This lesson was painful because Stanley was describing exactly what Dan was experiencing.

Stanley continued. "This slump in listener attention is inevitable. There's no escaping it. People have a lot on their minds, and it's easy to drift. Every leader must be able to re-earn their listeners' attention just before a critical content point in the talk.

"Too many people don't consider listening carefully as part of their job, Dan. Your team sees themselves as analysts, as planners, or tax experts.

They don't have the phrase 'expert listener' in their job descriptions. Look at the waiters here. They're pros. They're the best at what they do or they wouldn't be here. Do you notice when they take a customer's order they don't write it down? You know why? Because they know how to listen. They know how to give customers their full attention. They've been trained to do it. Your team hasn't; that's why you need to make it easy for them."

Stanley added to the diagram, showing peaks of interest and circled the peaks.

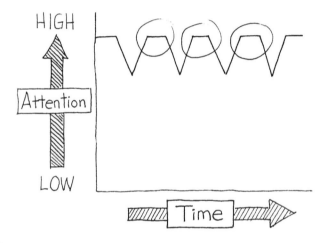

"As a leader, you must periodically create these peaks of interest to pull your listeners back into your talk just before you make a critical point. Get their attention."

Stanley clapped his hands right in front of Dan's face and hopped up. "Get their attention, then deliver the goods. After you've made your point, let up a bit. Let your listeners relax, then as you come to your next mission-critical point, grab their attention again. Every time you create peaks of interest and earn listeners' attention, you put them in a position to grow. Leaders do that; they put their people in positions to grow – that's part of what makes it easier for them to succeed," said Stanley.

Still smiling from Stanley's antics, Dan asked, "How do you earn their attention just at the right time?"

"There are many ways," said Stanley. "Humor, storytelling, metaphors, similes, colorful comparisons, audiovisual tools, movement, changes in your voice, gestures. We'll work on that. For now, I want you to understand that it's your responsibility – it's every leader's responsibility – to earn, then *re-earn* your listeners' attention. Don't cop the attitude that it's their job to listen to you. It's *your* job to make it easy for them to listen. If you don't, they won't."

"I don't know if I agree with that," said Dan. "My team has responsibilities and one of them is adopting a sense of ownership of our goals. Paying attention to me and what I'm saying during team meetings is a big part of that."

"Dan, it's not about you," said Stanley. "It's about normal but unacceptable human behavior. People drift off sometimes. Hell, Hollywood can't hold people's attention indefinitely. Don't think just because you're the boss that you're going to change that. What you *can* change is your ability to break through when you need to. Remember the professor from the leader speaker classification we talked about last time? Professors often think their brilliant content should be enough to hold people's attention. It isn't, and never will be. Remember this, Dan, every time you get up to speak, it's not about you. It's about dealing with the thousand little voices people have in their heads that compete with listening to you. You're not always going to be at the head of the line. Don't take it personally. That would be like getting mad at the sun for your sunburn. You can't change the sun, but you can roll over under the umbrella."

Dan still wasn't convinced his position as CEO was not a strong enough reason for people to pay attention to his every word. Hearing Stanley say, "It's not about you" didn't do it for Dan. *If leadership isn't about me, then who's it about?* thought Dan.

"Okay," said Dan, "give me a good example of earning attention."

"Have you seen the movie *Field of Dreams?*" asked Stanley.

Dan said, "Sure I did. That's where Kevin Costner played a farmer who built a baseball diamond in the middle of his corn field."

"That's right," said Stanley. "That farmer's name was Ray. Remember the scene near the end of the movie where he's on the pitcher's mound throwing fastballs to the catcher? After a few pitches, the catcher stands up and pulls off his mask. Do you remember who the catcher is?"

"It's his dad," answered Dan.

"Yes, his dad. When Ray was a teenager, he and his dad had a falling out and they didn't speak to each other for years. Then as Ray matured into his late twenties, they started to speak, but before they could reconcile and become like father and son again, his dad died."

"Dan, when I was a teenager, my dad and I stopped talking for a lot of stupid reasons," Stanley continued. "My dad never gave me credit for brains and never acknowledged what was important to me. Many years later, after I became a certified financial planner, my dad did an incredible thing: he asked me for help. He asked me to put together a financial plan for him. Do you know how much it meant to me to have my father acknowledge my competence and worthiness?"

As Stanley told his story, Dan was lost in his thoughts about his own story. Dan, too, had a rough relationship with his dad.

Stanley's question snapped Dan out of his daydream. "Yes, I do," said Dan.

Stanley said, "My dad and I set up an appointment for him to come to my office. I was ready to put all the pieces together for him. The day of his appointment, he arrived two hours late, which irritated me. He walked into my office soaking wet and shivering. It was February in Chicago and a miserable day. I asked him 'Hey, Rock, where have you been?' My brother and I had a nickname for our dad. We called him

Rock – it described his general attitude and flexibility on most topics.

"I got lost," he said.

"Lost? How do you get lost in Chicago? You've lived here all your life. And as I said this I noticed a look in my dad's eyes I'd never seen before. He was scared. I'd seen him mad many times, but never scared. He sat down, and, to make a long story short, we ended up taking him to Loyola Hospital, where he was hospitalized and treated for a stroke. He stayed in the hospital for several weeks. His discharge diagnosis included multiple strokes and early-onset Alzheimer's disease. For the next seven years my dad died one day at a time."

Stanley paused and took a moment.

Then he continued, "In *Field of Dreams*, when the catcher stands up and takes off his mask revealing Ray's dad, that movie has *earned* my attention. I'm not sitting there saying to myself that these are actors and this is a movie. No, I'm not *analyzing* things, I'm *feeling* things. Ray's dad is my dad. It has earned my full attention.

"When you speak, Dan, you need the equivalent of springing up out of your catcher's squat, pulling off your mask and drawing your listeners so close, they feel what you're saying. When they're feeling your words, I guarantee you, they're listening."

Stanley asked, "Tell me, Dan, what do you do now that earns your team's attention?"

"Apparently not enough, but I still don't think it's too much to ask well-paid adults to pay attention," said Dan, still annoyed that he should have to earn his team's attention.

Stanley fired back. "You're thinking a lot like many leaders I know who feel entitled to people's attention because of their leadership position. You can't pay to hold someone's attention for very long. It's not going to happen. You've proven that, haven't you?"

Dan felt Stanley's confidence and power. As he was about to respond, Stanley continued, "And what about the people who don't work for you? How are you going to earn their attention? You talk with clients, vendors, regulatory agencies, the press and your family. Hell, Dan, you speak to a lot more people who aren't on your payroll than are. How are you going to break through to them?"

"I don't remember too many people going way out of their way to make it easy for me to pay attention," Dan argued. "If I can pay attention I expect others to do so."

Stanley looked at Dan for a moment like a hunter waiting for the right moment to pull the trigger.

"I wonder if Steelman has that same attitude?" asked Stanley.

Dan flinched. Stanley knew full well the sting of this question.

Steelman. Nick Steelman was CEO of Empire Financial Ventures, Dan's company's arch rival. Steelman. His company was sprinting away from the rest of the pack, setting industry-record earnings, and proliferating innovative product and service lines. Steelman. The new king of the financial services industry and the source of Dan's nightmares. Steelman. His investors were dancing, while Dan's were sending him ominous e-mails.

Dan was jolted and fired back. "I don't know or care anything about Steelman's attitudes."

Stanley returned fire. "I wonder how your team would respond if you asked questions they could feel – just like I did with you. Do you think you'd earn their attention? Do you think you'd break through?"

"I don't know," Dan answered.

"It's time to find out, Dan," said Stanley. "We're running out of time."

Chapter Eight
Some People Just Don't Get It

D an's meeting with Stanley left him with a sour aftertaste that lingered into the next day. He didn't like thinking of himself as a "professor." It triggered flashbacks of the half-dead academics he had endured in grad school. Nor did he like being told it was his responsibility to earn his team's attention. And the more he thought about Stanley telling him, "It's not about you," the more it felt like an all-for-one and one-for-all leadership article written by some bleeding-heart burnout who's cleansing his soul by confessing corporate America's sins.

What really got to Dan was Stanley rubbing Steelman in his face. He was sick of hearing about Steelman. Steelman made Dan feel like the second-place finisher – the one the crowd shares a heartbeat of disappointment with for just before they leap to their feet and cheer the real winner. So far in the head-to-head competition with Steelman, Dan hadn't won a single medal.

And topping it all off, Stanley telling him, "We're running out of time" felt like pressure. He had enough pressure without more being dumped on him by some retired guy drinking a beer. Dan thought, *It's not "we" who are running out of time, it's me. Stanley's living large with nothing but time. I'm the guy with the vise crushing my head.*

Thankfully, the hustle of the day took Dan's mind off Stanley. His last meeting was with his marketing team. Dan had prepared his opening remarks a few days earlier, but at the last minute, while he was finishing up some business with Julie, she asked if he was ready for the marketing team meeting.

"Yes, I am," said Dan. "I'm opening with the last quarter's figures, then giving them my ideas on what we can do to pump them up."

Julie didn't say a word at first, then she asked, "How long do you think you can hold their attention with that?"

Dan bristled at her question, thinking she was Stanley's accomplice, then said, "Julie, I'm very well prepared for this meeting – I can handle it."

Dan's meeting with marketing lasted one hour. When it was over, Dan was exhausted and disappointed – much more than usual. As Dan walked back to his office, he fumed, *It's happened too many times now. People just don't get it. They don't have the big picture on things. It's like they haven't heard anything I've been talking about.*

They haven't heard anything I've been talking about. That thought stopped Dan's one-man bitch session. He could hear Stanley's voice telling him the same thing. *What if Stanley is right?* thought Dan. *What if they're not paying attention at a level they feel what I'm saying?* As Dan's thoughts grew stronger, he found himself almost talking out loud until he passed Julie, who was leaving for home as he walked into his office.

"How did it go?" asked Julie, breaking Dan's trance.

Seeing Julie at this moment was just what Dan needed.

"Not great," said Dan. "Did Stanley call today?"

Julie smiled. "Yes, he did and he asked me if you could meet him this evening. I told him yes, unless he heard differently."

"Good," said Dan. "I can use a drink."

Chapter Nine
Connection

Dan waited for Stanley at a table in the back room at The Red Head Piano Bar on Ontario Street. Dan remembered spending a week there one night in grad school.

Stanley was 30 minutes late. *Not like him*, Dan thought. *And why this place?* It was filling up with people and smoke and was getting noisy. Dan was still irked about having to earn the attention of his team. And there was something about Stanley saying, "It's not about you" that he still didn't like. With that thought, Dan heard the piano bar spring to life. The piano player started with "Tiny Dancer" – a reliable crowd pleaser. Dan walked up front, thinking he'd give Stanley a few more minutes before leaving. Just then, he saw Stanley walk in, pull up a stool at the piano bar, and wave him over.

"You're late," said Dan.

"I know and I'm sorry," said Stanley. "I got some bad news today. I chose this place because it always cheers me up."

Before Dan could ask about the bad news, Stanley was ordering drinks and stuffing 10-dollar bills into the glass next to the piano player's ashtray.

By now the piano player had most of the people at the bar singing along with him, *"Oh, ballerina, you must have seen her, dancing in the sand."*

"Do you know the difference between coming here and listening to this guy or going to a concert?" Stanley asked.

Dan was thinking there were about a hundred differences, but before he could say anything, Stanley answered his own question.

"The difference is this guy looks you in the eye as he's singing to you. He's singing to you, not just singing the song like at a concert. He's connecting with us. Sitting at this bar is a personal experience, at a concert, it's a performance. Here, it's more about us, at a concert, it's all about the singer. Here, it's a *relationship*, at the concert, it's a *recital*."

Dan knew there was a message in this for him.

"Did you bring paper?" asked Stanley.

As Dan handed the paper to Stanley, he got up and led Dan to a table at the rear of the bar where they could hear each other.

Stanley began. "Remember the peaks of interest I talked about last time? Tonight, I want to start showing you how to create the peaks.

"There's a process for creating peaks of attention. The process is like building a pyramid, where it's supported by a wide base. Tonight, we're going to talk about the base. The most fundamental aspect of creating peaks of attention is called connection."

Stanley drew a pyramid, divided it into four levels, and wrote "Connection" at the base.

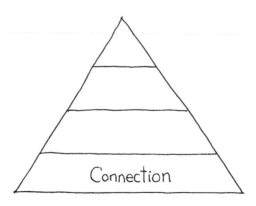

"I call this the leader's pyramid – it's how leaders create peaks of interest," said Stanley. "At its base is connection. Connection is when the listener feels they're having a personal experience with the leader speaker. Another word for connection is relationship. When we were sitting at that bar and the piano player sang directly to us, what did you experience?"

"I felt noticed. I felt important. Having someone sing directly to you is something that doesn't happen a lot," said Dan.

"That's right," said Stanley, "and having someone speak directly to you is something that doesn't happen a lot, either. Most leader speakers scan the room when they speak. They don't speak directly to anyone for any significant length of time. They make eye contact with you, but it's rarely enough to create any sense of relationship or personal impact."

"But that's not the advice my public speaking coach gave me," Dan said. "She said to try to make eye contact with everyone in the room, but don't spend too much time on any one person."

Stanley laughed. "Be careful of the advice you hear from presentation-skills trainers. Although they do well teaching how to present information, speaking like a leader is more than that. Even the phrase 'public speaking' is wrong for leaders. Here's some great advice: The next time you have a team meeting, talk to one person at a time. Forget the concept of public speaking. Don't talk to audiences, talk to individuals. Think of it as having a lot of consecutive, one-on-one conversations."

Stanley asked, "Dan, do you ever get a little nervous right before you give a talk?"

"Yes, I do," said Dan. "My presentation-skills coach told me I can overcome my nervousness by proper rehearsal, and by looking at the back of the room – not directly at my audience."

Stanley rolled his eyes and took a big swig of his drink.

"First of all, Dan, you're never going to get over being a little nervous before a talk. It's natural and good. You want some energy flowing in your veins before you start. Don't tell yourself you wish you weren't nervous. You're making yourself wrong right from the start, and that's the wrong kind of energy. Rehearsal never eliminated nervous energy for me or for a lot of leaders I know. In fact, too much rehearsal will create paralysis and dull your impact. Everyone can tell when someone is delivering a memorized speech. It's the quickest way to numb people's minds."

Stanley continued. "Connecting with an audience, talking to individuals in complete thoughts rather than just making fleeting eye contact will do a couple of things for you: First, it holds listeners' attention. When you speak directly to them and they know it, I guarantee you, they're listening, and, in many ways, you're honoring their presence. I recommend you hold the connection through complete thoughts. Don't change connection; that is, don't speak to someone else until you come to a natural punctuation point. That means you may speak several sentences to one person. When you do this, your listeners will notice your style. Those who you're not speaking directly to at that moment know that it will soon be their turn, which holds their attention.

"Another thing connection does is it helps you speak through your nervousness. Before you start your talk, pick out four friendly people in your audience – two on each side of the room – and plan connecting only with them during the first few minutes. You see, it's in the first few minutes when you feel your nerves the most. Planning your connections with listeners who give you good vibes increases your confidence and helps you sound leader-like early in your talk. Connection helps you sound like you're having a conversation with the audience, which is the most authentic and influential tone. After your butterflies are gone, then start connecting with the rest of the audience. Believe me, no one will notice you only spoke to four people during the first few minutes, they will notice your confidence."

By now, The Red Head was packed. Stanley fit right into the crowd with his bomber jacket and black mock-turtleneck. Dan was amused at

Stanley's dapper way of dressing. *A cool old guy*, Dan thought.

"There's another way to connect, another way to give your listeners the sense of a personal experience with you," said Stanley. "It's called disclosure. Disclosure is when your listeners get to know your secondary roles; that is, they get to know the person you are outside of your primary work role. For example, outside your work role of CEO, you're also a parent, a son, a golfer, a husband, and, unfortunately, you're a White Sox fan."

"Let me guess," said Dan. "You're a Cubs fan?"

"Not only that, Dan," replied Stanley, "I like ballroom dancing. I had a job as a busboy growing up, I hate sushi and root against all West-Coast professional teams. You see, Dan, our lives are so much more than our work roles. People need to know who they're following. Your team needs to know who you are. Disclosure does that."

"So are you saying I need to tell my team about my personal life?" Dan asked. "I don't know if I'm comfortable with that. I've always kept some strong boundaries between work and personal life."

"I agree," replied Stanley. "I like clear boundaries, too, but what I'm talking about here is letting people see the side of you that's more human and less corporate – especially parts of your life that are less than perfect. As leaders, Dan, we're forced many times in the public sector to keep our game faces on. With our teams, however, we need to create a sense that we're more alike than we are different. When people look at you, Dan, they see a good-looking, rich guy with an outstanding record of success and a perfect life. Your team can't relate to you on this level.

"What your team needs to learn about is where you fell and got up again. They need to learn about your hardships and flaws that are part of your life. Part of being a great leader means revealing the truth about yourself. Give them a keyhole to look into your life. In fact, it's the truth about you people need to see to grow. Your team can identify more with your flaws than your successes. Let them see a little bit of themselves in you. That's a big part of breaking through."

"How do I do that?" asked Dan.

"One of the best ways to disclose is to use personal stories about when you were growing up," Stanley replied. "That's one thing everyone has in common – we all grew up."

"My mother had a story for everything," Stanley continued. "I remember one time I asked her why I needed to wash my hands before I went to school. She said, 'When I was a little girl, we were very poor. During winter, my father would send my brothers, Harry and Peter, and me to the railroad switching yard down the street where we grew up in Cicero. That's where they'd switch cars from one train to another. When the coal cars would get jarred, coal would fall out of the bottom of the hoppers onto the tracks. My brothers and I would struggle up the tall hill to the tracks, crawl under the coal cars, pick up the coal, put it in paper bags and take it home, where my dad would use it to heat the house – and we weren't the only families doing this.' My mother said you could always tell who the poor kids were because they had dirty hands. 'Wash your hands, Stanley, we don't want people thinking we're poor.'"

There was something magical in the way Stanley told a story. Stanley's tale brought back memories of when Dan was in grade school and how, when he had a bandage on his finger, it would always come off when he'd wash his hands after recess. Stanley's stories reminded Dan of his own long-forgotten stories, and it felt good.

"So, how do I start connecting to people?" asked Dan.

Stanley liked this question and smiled when he answered.

"At your next meeting, begin thinking about making sustained eye connection. Talk to individuals, not to the group. You'll notice an immediate change in how you present yourself and how people respond to you. As far as disclosure is concerned, think about an event in your life, preferably when you were growing up, that somehow relates to your topic. Keep your story short – no more than 30 seconds. Use it early in your talk, and link it to your topic."

Stanley was all smiles. He felt Dan was getting into it.

"I've got to run," said Stanley, as he put on his jacket and tossed a five-dollar tip on the table. "I'll be in touch."

Dan drove home thinking about his lesson . As he pulled into his driveway, he remembered he had forgotten to ask Stanley about his bad news.

Chapter Ten
Progress

It was a week after Dan's piano-bar meeting with Stanley. Julie noticed Dan waltzing back to his office with a big smile on his face. He looked better than he had in months.

"You look like you just won the lottery," said Julie.

"I did," smiled Dan. "I just had a great meeting with my team. It's nice when everyone starts tugging on the rope in the same direction."

Dan and Julie returned to his office where he asked Julie to join him for a minute.

"Last week, Stanley taught me about connection using sustained eye contact and disclosure using short personal stories," Dan began. "I went home and told Diane about it, and she liked it so much, she helped me put together a few stories about when we were newlyweds living on a tight budget and raising a newborn. I used one of the stories as my opening with the team. I talked about our new customer service projects. I compared it to surviving being a newlywed, in that sometimes you get the unexpected, but with the right intentions and good communication, you can make something wonderful happen. What is really great was my team played off my story with stories and examples of their own. I could really feel the team coming together."

Julie beamed at Dan, saying, "I know. I got an e-mail from a few of the planners, and they said things went great. Whatever you're up to, keep doing it."

"Stanley talked to me about making sustained eye contact," Dan continued. "I realized I couldn't do that if everyone was staring at my presentation slides. So instead, I provided very simple handouts, and made notes to myself on my copy to keep me on track. The meeting evolved in a direction it probably wouldn't have if I had steered the group with my presentation slides agenda. Plus, we were able to look at each other more as we spoke, which made a huge difference in the room's energy. To top things off, you know Bob – the guy who deals in compliance issues – the one who is always the dark cloud in the room? Well, he comes up to me after the meeting and tells me a little story about his wife and their early days of marriage. He actually smiled when he was telling it. I thought his face was going to crack."

Julie said, "I love it, Dan. Stanley would be proud, and speaking of Stanley, he left you a voice mail."

Julie left Dan's office as he retrieved his message.

"Hey, Dan, it's Stanley. I'm on the Ferris wheel at Navy Pier and thinking about the other night at The Red Head. I forgot to tell you, 'What works at work, works at home.' Breaking through is about a lot more than just making a buck. Food for thought, my boy."

Chapter Eleven
Movement

When Julie told Dan about his next meeting place with Stanley, he was puzzled.

"Tell me again where he wants to meet?" said Dan.

"The Shubert Theater at four this afternoon," Julie said. "He says not to be late because you two are going to have to get off the stage by five. That's when rehearsals start." Julie was obviously amused by Stanley's methods.

By 3:45, Dan was entering the Shubert Theater through its backstage entrance when he saw Stanley pulling up and parking right behind his car. Stanley was driving a silver and black XJ-8 Jaguar.

Why am I not surprised? thought Dan.

"You look good in that car, Stanley," said Dan.

"Thanks, I just got it. I had to trade in my Porsche. It was too low for me. It felt like my butt was rubbing on the pavement," Stanley said.

Dan noticed Stanley always had an upbeat way of starting conversations. No dull, "So how have you been?" openers for Stanley, always a breath of fresh air.

The two walked in the back door of the theater. Stanley walked into an office and came out with a bright young woman who led them up some stairs, around rows of costume racks, and onto the main stage. She unclipped her cell phone, said a few words, and like magic, the overhead stage lights came on. Those lights felt good!

Stanley asked, "Do you like theater, Dan?"

"Yes, I do," said Dan. "Diane and I saw *The Producers* last year in New York."

"When you walked on this stage, did you notice the short strips of tape everywhere?" asked Stanley.

"I did, but I don't know what they're for," answered Dan.

"They're called blocking points," Stanley said. "They mark specific places on the stage actors need to be. Directors pay a lot of attention to how actors move and where they stand because movement and position influence how audiences perceive the performance. The stage has two basic areas: downstage and upstage. Downstage is close to the audience, upstage is toward the back of the stage, near the scenery. Both downstage and upstage are divided into center, left and right. So in the course of a play, the stage direction may call for the actor to start a line upstage left and cross to downstage right."

As Stanley was speaking, he walked to the upstage left position, and moved to downstage right, demonstrating his point.

Dan wanted to say, "Stanley, what could this possibly have to do with me?" but having been Stanley's student for a couple of weeks now, he knew he was trying to make a point.

"Actors move with purpose," said Stanley. "Movement is part of the play; they rehearse it. In many ways, movement is language, it communicates to the audience what words can't, or it adds depth of meaning to their words. It's no different with leader speakers. When you speak, your movement is part of your language. For leaders, the one thing movement signals more than anything is confidence."

"Are you suggesting that I rehearse my movements?" asked Dan.

"You bet," said Stanley. "Movement is one of the things that will hurt you more than help you. When it's done right, it won't make a bad talk good, but when it's done wrong it can make an otherwise good talk bomb. Have you ever had a speaker drive you nuts with the way they move?"

"Many times," said Dan. "A manager in our tax department paces too much. In fact, it makes me nervous to listen to him. Then there's Rita in marketing, who can't talk unless she's pushing her hair back."

"When you listen to these two people, what message does their movement send to you?" asked Stanley.

"They're nervous," said Dan.

"How does that reflect their confidence about what they're saying?" asked Stanley.

"Well, if they're nervous, maybe they're not confident at all," answered Dan.

"How ready are you to follow advice from a person who gives off vibes that lack confidence. And a bigger question, does a person who lacks confidence earn your attention?" asked Stanley.

"I see your point now. If my movement signals lack of confidence or sends a mixed message in any way, my listeners may be reluctant to act on what I'm saying, or, for that matter, not even pay attention," said Dan.

"Most of your leadership speaking will occur in a conference room with a small group, or one-on-one situations, or over the telephone," Stanley explained. "In these situations you're seated, and you're not going to move much. In small group and one-on-one settings, your connection and voice dynamics carry the load relative to breaking through. Over the telephone, it's all voice dynamics. However, there will be many occasions when you'll speak to a large group while standing, and movement has a major impact on your ability to break through."

"You're right," said Dan. "Our public relations team is putting me in front of more investor and community groups. We've also created a DVD as part of our identity package to investors. I saw some of the unedited version, and I thought I looked stiff and uncomfortable. Plus, I'm doing more media interviews now, and that's when I really need to shine."

"Good, you got the point," said Stanley. "Now, let's practice how to move. But remember, these techniques apply to any situation when you are standing and presenting or talking, not only on a stage."

Stanley walked to downstage center and said, "This is the most important place on the stage. It's the power position. When you speak, it puts you close to listeners. Your opening and closing remarks and all strong content are made here. Do your best never to give this space away. Too many leader speakers relinquish this space to an LCD or overhead projector. If you need a projector, position it with the screen placed at stage left or right or, better yet, use rear projection."

Stanley continued. "To the left and right of this center stage area are good spots for illustrative content, like stories. Also, you want to use the left and right side of the room to connect with people who are sitting on those sides. As a leader, you're not going to use the upstage positions, which are away from your listeners, much. So let's focus on how to move from the center to the left, to the right, and back to the center."

Stanley positioned Dan at center stage and said, "There are four steps to moving with confidence. Don't worry about remembering this right now, you can make notes later. The first step of confident movement is no movement at all. By movement, I mean traveling from one area of the stage to another. I'm not talking about gestures or upper-body motions when I refer to movement. Gestures occur naturally, nearly all the time, and that's fine.

"For example, you're at center stage now. If you want to move to the left, first become still. That way, when you do move, your movement creates contrast. This makes the movement appear purposeful. If you're constantly moving while you speak, nothing seems purposeful, and it's exhausting to your listeners.

"The second step to moving with confidence is to connect with someone. To make it easy for now, think about connecting with someone in the direction you're planning to move.

"The third step is to hold the connection for a meaningful period of time before you move. When you do move, hold the connection as you're moving to your destination.

"The fourth step to moving with confidence is to stop moving and change connection when you reach your destination."

As Stanley explained confident movement to Dan, he demonstrated the process. What was interesting to Dan was how Stanley had a light stride, almost floating as he moved. Then Dan remembered that Stanley liked ballroom dancing.

"It looks like your dancing has influenced how you move on stage," said Dan.

"Thanks. Dancing is good preparation for leader speakers," replied Stanley. "Good posture and easy, purposeful movement all contribute to leader-like stature. Leader speakers who slouch and wander around with no purpose in their movement don't have nearly the presence or breakthrough they could have."

Dan asked, "What about gestures? Do you have a formula for them, too?"

"Heck, no," said Stanley. "The worst thing you can do is get hung up thinking about what to do with you hands and arms. Gestures are natural movements that take place in response to the emotion and energy you feel as you speak. Do what comes naturally, and you'll be right. I enjoy leader speakers who speak with their whole bodies. Don't confuse movement and gestures. Movement is traveling across the stage; gestures are upper-body motions that are part of your speaking personality. Keep your movement to a minimum, but when you do move, do it purposefully; no pacing, wandering or drifting. Let the energy of your talk drive your gestures. Be conservative with movement and liberal with gestures."

For the next 30 minutes, Stanley and Dan worked on movement. At first, it seemed stiff and rehearsed to Dan, but as he got into it, it came easily.

"This is nice," said Dan. "I never thought about movement, but now that I've done it, I can see it makes a big difference. It actually feels good to do it right."

Stanley and Dan finished their session and walked out to their cars. Dan pulled out some paper and made some notes.

"Here, let me show you something," said Stanley as he reached for Dan's notes. "Here's how movement fits into the leader's pyramid."

Stanley drew the leader's pyramid. He wrote "Connection" on the base, then added "Movement" right above it.

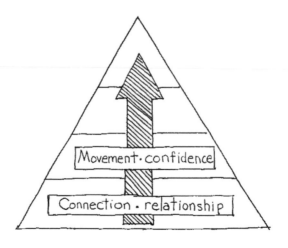

"Do you remember this?" asked Stanley.

"Sure I do. You drew this last time we were at the piano bar."

"Good," said Stanley. "This pyramid illustrates the process for breakthrough. It rests on a wide base. That's connection. Another way to think about connection is relationship. You build breakthrough from the base up. Your first focus as a developing leader speaker should be on connection. Master it. Never give another talk without it. Then, after you don't have to think about connection and you do it automatically, get conscious about your movement. Movement will be the easiest thing I teach you about breaking through. Just remember: conservative movement and liberal gestures, and you'll be fine."

The two men walked to their cars. Stanley started his, punched on some music, and put his convertible top down. He pulled out next to Dan.

Dan rolled down his window and said, "You seem to really know your stuff. When do I get to hear you speak? I'd like to see you in action." In a flash, Dan could see the light in Stanley's eyes darken and his buoyant mood sink.

"The day will come when you'll see everything I know in action," said Stanley.

"When will that be?" asked Dan.

"I'm not sure, but I have a feeling it will be soon. Too soon," said Stanley as he disappeared into traffic.

Chapter Twelve
Perplexed

The next day, Dan was perplexed as to why Stanley's mood had crashed the night before. The two were having such a good time strutting across the stage, then Stanley's spirit suddenly darkened. Dan couldn't think of a thing he had done to bring Stanley down.

As Dan finished the morning with his estate-planning team, he saw Julie leaving for lunch.

"Julie, do you have a minute? I have a question about Stanley," said Dan.

"Sure," beamed Julie, as the two of them walked into Dan's office.

"Stanley did something odd yesterday," Dan said. "We had a great session together, but as we were leaving, I asked him when I'd get to hear him speak. After I asked him, I noticed a dramatic shift in his mood."

"How did he answer your question?" Julie asked.

"He said that someday I'd see his work in action, or something like that. I could tell I must have done something very wrong," said Dan.

Julie had the best poker face in Chicago. She'd learned how to smile through the worst of times and at the biggest jerks in business, but Dan could see in her eyes that he had just dealt her an unwanted card.

Julie took a moment. "It could be that it's not about you." She stood and excused herself, saying she was running late for a lunch meeting, forced a smile, and left.

Chapter Thirteen
Dynamics

W hen the seasons change in Chicago, so do its people. This year was no different. Summer was over, the days were growing shorter, and like always, Dan was dreading late fall's blanket of gray skies that snuffed out the city's last flicker of summer life. He also was dreading the possibility of poor year-end earnings reports. His earnings were flat, and he needed some big numbers to make up for his spring losses. Like the weather, Dan's attitude and activity were growing more brisk. Change was in the air.

Dan and his team had launched several new products and upgraded some key client-services activities. Things were looking better. His days were filled with meetings, and not one went by without his remembering Stanley's advice on breaking through. Since their first meeting, Dan kept a pocket notebook journal in his desk. He'd transfer his notes from bar napkins and yellow notepad paper to his journal. It helped him remember. He would often debrief team meetings in his journal. He'd list what went right, what could have been better, and how he used the concepts of earning attention, connection, minimizing the knowledge gap and movement. His journal calmed him as he found himself becoming more conscious as a leader speaker and more in control of himself and the outcomes. He felt less like a victim of complex communications environments and more like a leader. It began to feel like he was breaking through.

One morning, Dan was about to check his e-mails when Julie walked in and said he had a call on line one.

"Hello, Dan, Stanley here. Do you have time today for a working lunch?" asked Stanley, who by the ring in his voice sounded like he was over his blue mood.

"I'm slammed today. How 'bout tomorrow?" replied Dan.

"Wrong answer; tomorrow may never come. *Carpe diem*, Danno. No time like the present," said Stanley, who was brimming over with spunk.

Stanley was talking so loudly that Julie, who was leaning against the doorway in Dan's office, could hear him. As Dan recited more reasons why a lunch was not possible today, Julie started shaking her head in disapproval, made throat-slashing gestures with her finger, and finally scratched out a note that read, "Have lunch with Stanley, I'll hold off the wolves!"

Dan smiled and said, "Okay, Stanley, I'll meet you for lunch. It seems like Julie thinks I'm better off with you than I am here running this company."

"Ah, sweet Julie," said Stanley. "Always the brightest bulb in the chandelier."

Dan and Stanley met at Portillo's – Beef, Burgers and Beer at Clark and Ontario streets, every Chicagoan's best-loved street-food joint. The place was mobbed. They got in line and ordered Italian beef sandwiches, onion rings and two tall beers, then found a table upstairs away from the hungry mob.

Stanley asked, "When we first walked in here, what did you immediately notice?"

"The people and the noise. This place is loaded and loud," answered Dan.

"I agree," said Stanley. "There's great energy in here. I think the energy in a restaurant is the key ingredient for a great experience. Have you ever walked into a dim, half-empty restaurant with slouchy waiters and felt your energy and mood sink? Restaurants with low energy go out of business. Leader speakers with low energy go out of business, too."

Leave it to Stanley not to waste a minute on small talk. Dan was just two bites into his sandwich when Stanley started his lesson. Dan put his sandwich down and pulled out his pocket journal to take notes.

"All right," said Stanley. "Nice notebook. Can I take a look?"

Dan handed Stanley his notes on all their previous meetings with his own comments alongside. Dan could tell Stanley was flattered and highly amused by Dan's notes, commenting on a few of them as he thumbed through the pages.

Stanley handed the journal back to Dan and said, "Let's talk about the energy of the leader speaker. Draw the leader's pyramid for me and label the first two levels."

Dan drew the pyramid and labeled the foundational level "Connection" and the next level up "Movement."

Stanley said, "Now remember, connection is about creating relationships and movement is about signaling confidence. The next level up on the pyramid is called dynamics. Dynamics is all about energy."

Dan added "Dynamics" to his leader's pyramid drawing.

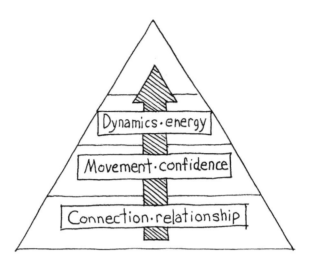

Stanley asked, "Dan, tell me what does the leader's pyramid represent?"

"It represents how the leader speaker can create the peaks of listener attention," answered Dan. "It's how leaders break through."

"That's right," said Stanley. "Let's talk about the third level: dynamics. Dynamics is the sound of your voice. It's what creates the energy people feel," explained Stanley. "Dynamics includes pitch, tone, volume, rhythm, crescendos, and the pace of your talk. Think of speaking like singing, except with narrower changes in pitch and no melody. Just about everything that applies to musical dynamics applies to the dynamics of the speaking voice."

Stanley asked, "Have you ever had a tune stick in your head you kept hearing?"

Dan smiled. "Yes, I have. I remember one time I was in a staff meeting and I couldn't get Peter Frampton's song, "Do You Feel Like We Do?" out of my head. It's the only thing I remember about that staff meeting!"

Stanley and Dan laughed, clicked beer glasses, and toasted to forgettable staff meetings.

"What if you could speak in a way so that your listeners couldn't get your tune out of their heads?" asked Stanley.

"Now that would be a trick," said Dan.

"You're right, it *is* a trick. It's like a magician pulling a rabbit out of the hat. The real talent is learning how to get the rabbit in the hat. Understanding the leader's pyramid is like learning how to put the rabbit in the hat. Learn that, and you'll have a much greater chance of your words sticking in your listeners' heads. It all goes back to earning attention.

"When composers write music, they use dynamic contrasts," Stanley continued. "Quiet passages followed by loud ones, short *pizzicato* punchy passages, followed by attached flowing ones. Without contrast, listeners would grow bored and stop listening, even though the music might still be playing. Your speaking is no different: Without dynamic contrasts, people will stop listening, even though your music is still playing."

Dan asked, "Give me an example of a dynamic contrast."

"A good example is speaking rate and pace," Stanley replied. "Rate is the number of words a minute you speak. In music, it's called tempo. Pace is the time interval of silence between thoughts. In music, it's called rhythm."

Then, as fast as he could, in one breath with no pauses between words, Stanley said: "It's-rare-that-people-speak-too-fast. We-can-hear-and-understand-words-that-are-delivered-at-a-blistering-speed.

"I call the speed I just used 'rate,'" said Stanley. "Now, I can talk at the same rate, but if I add pace, which is a pause between my main thoughts, you can listen to it just fine.

"It's-rare-that-people-speak-too-fast."

Stanley paused for just a heartbeat.

"We-can-hear-and-understand-words-that-are-delivered-at-a-blister-ing-speed."

Stanley said, "Leader speakers make mistakes in respect to pace, or pauses. And I hesitate to use the word pause because it suggests there's a loss of energy. Just the opposite is true. When done right, pauses boost energy and earn attention."

"My wife has a realtor friend who, once she starts, won't stop talking. We bought our home from her. By the end of it, I wanted to shoot myself," Dan said.

"Here's the real power of the pause," said Stanley. "Listeners learn during the silence. People grow during the silence. People make decisions during the silence. In many ways, you lead during the silence. You break through during the silence. The best leader speakers know when to become silent and let what they've said sink in.

"For example, when you're talking to your team and you see them taking notes, pause a bit and let them finish. I do that with you, if you've noticed."

"I have, and when you do, I don't feel rushed taking notes," Dan replied. "I sense it's more important to you that I learn something, than it is for you to keep talking."

"Give your team the same experience," said Stanley. "You'll find people will experience a greater depth of understanding and confidence when you honor the time they need to record their thoughts with your silence. It's a very leader-like thing to do."

Stanley continued. "The whole idea of dynamic contrasts is to earn attention. Know the critical content of your talk that your listeners must get, then just before and after you deliver the critical content, change your dynamics. Wrap your key content in dynamic contrast. Surround a target word or phrase with contrasting dynamics.

"Let's say the concept you want your listeners to really hear is xylophone. Just before you say it, pause or get louder, or softer, or raise or lower your pitch, speak with an accent, or whatever you need to do to change the sound of your voice. The change re-earns their attention, and then, you deliver your key concept.

"That's why humor in leadership is so important. Humor is one of the best ways to earn attention. Get them laughing, then just as the laughter ends, deliver your message. Works like a charm every time! The only thing more important than humor is oxygen."

Stanley paused, stood up, looked directly into Dan's eyes, lowered his voice, and said, "One thing I absolutely know about speaking like a leader is you must earn attention immediately before delivering your key concepts."

Dan smiled, "Well done, Stanley."

"One more thing," said Stanley. "Just like the high-energy sound in this place, so much of what you feel is created through what you hear. The melody and lyrics of an old love song spawn feelings long forgotten. It's the sound of your voice, not the meaning of your words, that help people feel your words. Let me be quick to add here, I'm not saying the meaning of your words, which I call content, can't affect how people feel. It does, but an additional language piece your listeners can experience – beyond the meaning of your words – is the feeling of your words. Words conjure up feelings, as well as meaning. Breaking through requires dealing with the meaning and *feeling* of words. And it's the sound of the words – the sound of your voice – that transfers what you're feeling about your content to your listeners. The best leader speakers get their listeners to feel like they do. That's a big part of what helps listeners take action in the direction of your vision."

"I've got to believe if my team felt as I do, things would be a lot different," Dan said.

"How so?" asked Stanley.

"The big difference would be commitment," Dan answered. "People would do what they've been trained to do because they'd *feel* like doing it. They'd be inspired, engaged, and give their jobs extra effort. Plus, I believe if people felt about their work as I do, we'd have greater loyalty and less turnover. Losing people must be about them not feeling good about what they're doing."

"Of course it is," said Stanley. "Feel great about what you do. Sound like it, and your people will respond to you."

As they were leaving, Stanley said, "I'll walk with you part of the way," and with that, he set a quick pace down Clark Street. It took Dan three big strides to catch up, which got him thinking he would have to work to keep up with Stanley. Stanley kept leading the way, and at the next intersection, he broke into a trot to beat the traffic light. Dan followed.

"There's another thing dynamics will do for you," said Stanley. "When you get behind your voice and really express yourself with passion; you'll find your energy increases. Your heart beats faster, your blood surges through your brain. You feel more alive. It's just like this quick hike we're taking now. Do you feel your metabolic rate increase? Do you feel the surge?"

Dan laughed. "Yeah, I do. I'm waiting for you to start sprinting any second." Dan thought, *This guy's in great shape*.

Stanley smiled and asked, "Dan, have you ever given a talk when out of the blue, comes a completely original thought, one you never related to your content?"

"Yes, I have," said Dan, who was becoming short of breath.

"I call those moments of clarity," said Stanley. "I'm convinced that moments of clarity – original thoughts – are facilitated by increased metabolic rate. Have you ever taken a walk thinking about some issue, when all of a sudden your thinking about this issue became clearer?"

"Sure, walking and exercise seem to clear my mind," said Dan.

"Okay," said Stanley. "You know what I'm talking about. When you express yourself with energy, it's like taking a walk. It pumps up your metabolism and clears your mind, making room for original thoughts."

Stanley continued. "Another factor in moments of clarity is what I call expressed thinking. When an author sits down to write, she engages in inner-directed thinking. She's talking to herself when she writes. If she doesn't like it, she can backspace it out of existence. However, when you stand up to speak, there's no taking it back. Speaking is outer directed, or expressed thinking: people know immediately what you're thinking because you say it. There's a risk in expressed thinking; there's an edge to it. That edge combined with the buzz normally associated with speaking in front of a group, along with increased metabolic rate, takes you to a higher state of consciousness. Athletes call it being in the zone. In many ways you become smarter, more alert, and more aware as you speak, and able to access thoughts you can't access when you're at a lower level of consciousness."

"So are you saying if I speak with more energy – greater dynamic distinctions – that I may get clearer in my thinking and have more original thoughts?" Dan asked.

"Absolutely yes," said Stanley. "Early in my leadership career I noticed the relationship between dynamic delivery and moments of clarity. After a while, I began to expect moments of clarity and kept a notepad handy while speaking. Otherwise, I found moments of clarity were easy to forget. The big jump for me was when I went into every talk with the intention of creating moments of clarity. I got to the point I knew by the end of my talk I'd understand more about my topic. The next time I spoke on this topic or a related one, I'd include the moment of clarity I'd experienced previously, making my current talk that much better.

"Remember how I said creating the peaks of interest puts your listeners in a position to grow?" Stanley continued. "What I learned was this: creating peaks of interest using an expressive delivery put me in a position to grow."

Stanley stopped walking, sat on a bus bench and motioned for Dan to sit next to him.

Stanley asked, "Dan, what would it mean if every time you spoke you were a little bit better than the previous time?"

Dan smiled. "If that were the case, my ability to speak like a leader would compound, just like money. If I could be just one or two percent better every time I lead a talk, over time, it would yield a huge improvement."

Stanley asked, "What would improve?"

"My impact," answered Dan.

Stanley flinched. "Yes, that's true, but what's the outcome of that? What end does your improved impact serve?"

Dan was stuck.

Stanley said, "Let me give you a hint: It's not about you."

There it was again: "It's not about you." Dan hated hearing that. He'd heard it before, and hearing it again didn't take him anywhere other than down. It felt like he was being called selfish. This was not his intention, and he resented hearing it.

Stanley sensed Dan's discomfort, but held off saying anything for just a moment, then asked, "What do leaders do?"

The question brought Dan back. "Leaders create environments where it's easy for people to succeed and ... "

Stanley interrupted and finished his answer, " ... help people feel better about themselves."

Dan relaxed and thought for a moment, then said, "Okay, I get it. As my impact as a leader speaker improves, this makes it easier for people to succeed and feel better about themselves."

"Bingo," smiled Stanley. "Here's a subtlety I don't want you to miss. All along, I've talked about how critical it is to earn your listener's attention and break through, but you don't want to do it in a way that diminishes your listener. For example, once we held our annual meeting in Reno. Our events coordinator hired an opening session speaker who rode out onto the stage on a 10-foot-tall unicycle while juggling bowling pins. As he rode around, he drew comparisons between us and him, saying how we had to juggle things, balance priorities and take risks. We were all amazed, but after watching him for a few minutes, his act got in the way of his message. After a short while his message began to feel like, *Look at me: I can do this and you can't.* Our attention was on him – wondering – some of us hoping – when he'd fall off that thing. His presence – his ability to hold our attention – was all about him, not about us. It was not authentic.

"Being authentic is a key issue," Stanley continued. "Authentic presence is when you earn attention in a way listeners see some of themselves in you; your message becomes personal to the listener. Authentic presence is manifested when their attention is on you initially, then migrates to their own inner dialogues and images. This helps them see and feel themselves aligning to the vision you've helped create. When your presence is authentic, your vision can become a shared vision.

"Great storytellers do a similar thing. A great story frees the imagination and spawns images and feelings within the listener, making the storyteller almost invisible. Great movies do the same. Great movies and great stories free us up to see and feel what we have inside. Authentic presence frees up your listeners to see and feel what they have inside. When you can do that is when you break through."

As Stanley spoke, his voice carried and a small group formed around the bench, as if Stanley and Dan were street musicians playing for tips. Dan was unaware of the group because he was lost in his own thoughts. When Stanley finished speaking, no one in the crowd spoke, hoping there would be more. The silence continued. Then finally, a woman urged, "Tell us more."

Stanley smiled at her, looked at Dan, then said, "Ask this young man here. It's my time to go."

Chapter Fourteen
Challenge

As Dan returned to his office following his lunch with Stanley, Julie spotted him in the lobby waiting for the elevator. She stepped up her pace and reached him as the elevator's door slid shut and launched the elevator to the top floor.

"How's Stanley?" asked Julie.

"Good," smiled Dan. "He has some amazing insights into leadership. We ended up walking back part of the way together, and he actually drew a little crowd talking about his ideas."

Julie said, "Stanley loves to talk about leadership speaking. He started a leader speaker mentoring program here years ago, and he'd give talks about once a week. They were great. I sat in on all of them."

"Really?" replied Dan as they got off the elevator and headed toward Dan's office. "Then you must know some of the things Stanley's telling me."

"I do, and I hope I haven't forgotten too much. After a few sessions with Stanley, I suggested he offer a similar program for the administrative staff. Stanley jumped on the idea and asked me if I'd lead it. At first I thought I didn't know the concepts well enough, so Stanley spent extra time with me. Between the two of us, we ended up with something everyone enjoyed, while boosting their spirits. Stanley and I knew the administrative support staff spent more time talking with clients than the planners. We figured, why not teach them to speak like leaders? It turned out to be a big hit with everyone. The team was jazzed about it, the clients responded, and we kept on making nice profits. Stanley always emphasized the importance of helping people feel good about themselves and to look for ways to make it easy for them to succeed. Stanley was really clear on the distinction between helping people feel good about themselves versus schmoozing them. He made sure the administrative support teams knew it, too. Stanley helped me lead the entire effort, and in the process made my job a blast."

"How did the administrative staff like it?" Dan asked.

"They loved it," said Julie. "I'll tell you what team members respond to, Dan, they love being in the loop. They want to know what's going on, they want to be part of the action. Being part of the action stretches people. The good ones grow stronger, and team members who don't grow, leave. When you engage people, when you stretch them, they'll reveal their intentions. In the presence of challenge, those who intend to excel, do. Challenge your team long enough, and what you end up with are all the winners; the losers have moved on to safer jobs where they can hide. Stanley had a great way of saying this. He'd ask us, 'Do you know why Sneezy of the Seven Dwarfs whistles while he works? Because the other six are,' which was Stanley's way of saying, 'If you're not whistling, others will notice.' Challenging the administrative staff to speak like leaders really stretched them and eventually created the strongest team I've ever worked with."

Dan smiled as Julie spoke. He could see Stanley's influence on her, and it suited her well. Julie followed Dan into his office as they were finishing their conversation.

"Sounds like you've heard Stanley speak many times," said Dan. "Tell me about the best talk you heard him give."

Julie paused, then folded her arms.

"I'm going to give Stanley a little more time with you before I do. It's a great story," Julie said, smiling, then backed out of Dan's office and closed the door behind her.

Chapter Fifteen
Quick-Start Structure

The big day for Dan and his sales team was here. In two hours, the principals of Taylor Manufacturing would be in Dan's conference room. Taylor Manufacturing had billions in its pension fund, and was looking for a new fund manager. Dan and his team were going for this prize account, but unfortunately, he was drawing a blank thinking about his opening and closing remarks. Dan was stuck. His team had all the numbers and processes sorted out, so he wasn't worried about the technical side of the presentation. He was worried about the *personal* side. Taylor had been family owned for four generations. They looked you in the eye when they did business. Dan knew they were talking to other financial planning firms. He also knew their decision would be heavily influenced by the chemistry among the players. Dan was much better at financial planning than he was at chemistry.

As Dan stewed in his office, Julie buzzed him on the speakerphone and asked how it was going with the Taylor presentation.

"It's not," said Dan. "Everything I think about saying sounds like a cliché."

"I'll be right in," said Julie.

A heartbeat later, Julie walked into Dan's office where Dan was hunched over his notebook computer, and muttering at his presentation slides. He looked as if he had already lost the account.

"I wonder what advice Stanley would give you right now?" asked Julie, knowing this might not be what Dan wanted to hear.

"It might be too late for Stanley," said Dan. "I should have talked to him about this weeks ago."

"Let's try anyway," said Julie while wheeling out of Dan's office.

A minute later, Dan's phone buzzed. It was Stanley.

Stanley jumped right in. "You picked a hell of a time to get constipated over a presentation. What's your problem?"

"I'm not sure how to start the presentation, and I don't mean the hello and welcome stuff. I mean, how do you grab their attention from the get-go?"

"How much time do we have to work on this?" asked Stanley.

"A few minutes, then I have to meet with my team."

"Okay," said Stanley. "I'll give you the quick-start version of a talk we'll have some other time. Julie tells me you've got an hour and a half with them. Here's what I'd do: First, frame your opening remarks with this structure: What are we going to talk about; why are we talking about it; and why is it important *now*? What, why and why now? The 'what' is a one-, to two-sentence overview of your proposal. The 'why' focuses on the outcome of your processes. Don't confuse this with *how* you're going to do things. That's part of the technical presentation. Allow the 'why' to relate to the outcome Taylor Manufacturing wants. And let me say this: If you don't know their why, just shoot yourself now."

"We know the why," Dan said. "They want a broader asset allocation with minimal risks along with ... "

Stanley interrupted. "Spare me the details. I've been there before. Let's move on to the most important part of your introductory remarks, the 'why now' part. The 'why now' relates to the reason or reasons why Taylor is taking action now. Typically the 'why now' involves some crisis, or some opportunity, or fear, or some business cycle issues that move people to take action. Send a really clear message you get their reasons for 'why now.' Acknowledging people's 'why nows' is a great way to earn attention. It's at the heart of good leadership."

"Got it," said Dan, who was feeling much better. Dan knew the what, why, and why now. The "what," "why" and "why now" linked together in the introduction made great sense. What he didn't know was how to put them together.

Stanley continued. "The last thing I suggest you do in your introductory remarks is to foreshadow your call to action. Let me ask you this: What do you want them to do as a result of your presentation? What is the next step they take to align with your vision? That is your call to action. Foreshadow that. Allude to that in your opening remarks. You just finished your what, why and why now. Foreshadow your call to action by saying something like, '... and at the end of our recommendations today, I'm going to suggest you....' You demonstrate confidence when you tell them you can solve their problems before you tell them how."

As Stanley talked, Dan made notes in his journal. Hearing Stanley's advice on structure made perfect sense. Within moments, he had a good feel for what he'd say. It seemed to Dan when the structure was apparent, the words came more easily.

Stanley asked, "Did you know I pitched Taylor Manufacturing many years ago?"

"No, I didn't," said Dan. "It wasn't in their file."

"It wouldn't be," said Stanley. "I pitched old man Taylor, the grandson of the founder, in a tavern 15 years ago. We did business a lot differently then. You're dealing with his son today. I didn't get the account. Some discounter got it by shaving their margins. If I were you, I'd be prepared for him interrupting your technical presenters and redirecting questions or comments to you. They like to see what the leader is made of."

"Any advice here?" asked Dan.

"What always worked for me in sales presentations is imagining the client was part of my team. Then I'd apply the same rules of leadership to them as I do my employees – make it easy for them to succeed. In the sales environment, it means make it easy for them to buy, and make them feel better about themselves. I'm assuming you've made the buying process easy, so let's focus on them feeling better about themselves.

"I'd get really clear about what you want them to *know* and what you want them to *feel*. Getting clear about what you want them to know, I call the *teach* piece. Teach with handouts, projected graphics and lecture – one-way explanations. I'm sure your presentation covers all the bases in respect to what you want them to know. Where most talks fail is getting clear about what you want them to feel. I call this the *lead* piece. You're going to lead with your delivery: connection, movement, dynamics – the leader's pyramid. Do you remember the leader's pyramid?"

"Sure I do," said Dan.

"We completed the first three levels of the pyramid: connection, movement and dynamics. The last level, the level at the top, is content. Your content is supported by the three levels beneath it. Do you have your journal handy?" Stanley asked.

"Yes, I'm looking at it now," said Dan.

"Good," said Stanley. "Write 'Content' on the top level of the pyramid. Then, I want you to draw a line horizontally through the pyramid between the content and dynamic levels.

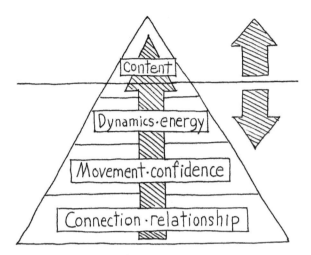

"Now, as you were creating your talk to Taylor, were you preparing above or below this line?"

"Above the line," said Dan.

"I know. Most leader speakers do. They rehearse their content. Guess what? You don't need to rehearse your content. You know it. You're an expert. Don't rehearse content, organize it. That's what handouts, overheads, presentation slides, and your technical presenters are for. What you need to rehearse is below the line: your delivery. It's your delivery that enables listeners to feel your words. What is it you want the Taylor group to feel, Dan?"

"I want them to feel confident in us. I want them to feel excited about working with us. I want them to like who we are and how we do business," replied Dan.

"Good answers," said Stanley. "Additionally, don't forget you want them to feel good about themselves and their decision to offer you the shot at getting their business. If you want them to feel confident in you, you must feel it as you speak. Emotions are contagious. If you're not jazzed, they'll never feel jazzed. If you want them to be excited, then you must have an edge of excitement in your presentation. People need to feel your words. If that's to happen, you must feel them first. Dan, have you ever watched a monkey climb a tree?"

"Yes, I have. They run right up the trunk."

"That's right," said Stanley. "Monkeys can climb trees without moving the branches. When bears climb trees, they break branches and bend the tree. When some leaders speak, they're like monkeys – they don't move the listeners. When the best leader speakers speak, they're like bears. They move their listeners; they bend trees and snap a few branches. Great leader speakers alter their listeners."

"I hear what you're saying," said Dan, "but I can't go overboard with too much emotion. I'll lose credibility, plus I've got to factor in compliance issues, political correctness, and all the corporate culture issues."

"You're right," said Stanley. "All that matters, and because of this it's tricky to be authentic in the corporate environment, especially one that's as highly regulated as the financial services industry. But what's happened is that the pendulum of correctness has swung too far. I've seen leader speakers who are so paranoid about their corporate image, they've lost their identity, their energy, and their personality in front of an audience. Their delivery is sterile, calculated and poorly read from soulless teleprompters, making them sound like talking dogs. Too many people jockeying for position leads to some very uninspiring talks that creates a difficult decision for the audience: whether to listen or to have their tonsils removed.

"Dan, let them feel what you feel. Be authentic. Remember what I told you the other day in Portillos – no one ever lost credibility by being interesting."

"You're right," said Dan. "I guess I was overthinking this Taylor presentation. We really need them to make our numbers shine."

"Yes, you do, but don't *sell* them, *lead* them. Present yourself in such a way that even if they don't buy, they'll never forget how they felt when you offered it. And who knows, the day may come when you'll find them at your door once again."

As Dan and Stanley said their goodbyes, Stanley said, "And by the way, I forgot one thing. In the beginning of your talk, tell a quick little story or give an example or comparison that ties into your topic. Something they don't expect. Don't be afraid to have fun when the chips are down. It will lighten your load. Good luck!"

Dan and Julie met with the presentation team shortly before Dan greeted the Taylor group. As they got comfortable in the conference room, introductions were made, coffee was served, and the group settled in. Dan rose, walked to the head of the long oval conference table, shot Julie a quick smile, and launched into his introduction.

"Thanks to you all for being here today. Your company, Taylor Manufacturing, has a rich history of success in the Midwest and we're flattered you're considering using our firm to manage your pension fund.

"Have you ever watched a monkey climb a tree?" Dan paused just long enough until every eye was on him.

"Monkeys can climb trees without moving the branches, the tree doesn't move. When bears climb trees, they break branches and move the tree, they bend the tree." As Dan said this, he tipped his body to the side as if he was a bending tree. The group smiled.

Then Dan connected directly with Taylor's CEO and said, "Our presentation today is going to bend your tree. It will alter the way you look at pension investing. It will break some of the branches called assumptions about the investing marketplace and how to be successful in it ..."

• • • • •

Two hours later, Dan was enjoying a walk outside across the State Street Bridge and replaying the presentation in his head. He smiled to himself while picturing how dialed in the group had been, how alert and responsive they were to his recommendations, how pumped his technical presentation team was, sensing they were feeding off his energy. It had been a great day.

Dan's cell phone rang. It was Stanley.

"How'd it go, my boy?" asked Stanley.

"We got it," cheered Dan. "The whole deal. Plus, they want to use us for their personal investing, insurance, the whole ball of wax. Stanley, I can't thank you enough."

The two talked for several minutes about the details of the deal. As they were ending their conversation Dan said, "You know, I used your monkey story. It went over great! I owe you a drink."

Stanley laughed. "Your timing is perfect. After you see tomorrow's *Tribune*, you'll need a drink, too."

"What's in tomorrow's newspaper?"

"A little reminder to continue to grow as a leader," answered Stanley. "I'll see you for my drink tomorrow."

Chapter Sixteen
Storytelling

The next day for Dan was a blur. Landing the Taylor account had kicked everyone and everything into high gear. Congratulatory phone calls and e-mails poured in. Winning the Taylor account was like a huge dose of caffeine that Dan and his team needed to kick-start their comeback. It looked like the third quarter numbers were going to shine. It felt good. And in the hustle of it all, Dan forgot about Stanley's comment about the newspaper.

It was late morning and Dan had just finished an "atta boy" conference call with a few of his board members that almost left him giddy. Then Julie snuck into his office as he hung up.

"Have you seen this yet?" asked Julie as she handed Dan the financial pages of *The Chicago Tribune*.

The lead article's headline read, "Steelman Brings Hope to the Homeless." The article went on to say how Nick Steelman, CEO of Empire Financial Ventures, was bringing area business leaders together to support community leaders in their efforts to help the homeless. The article was laden with accolades for Steelman, contrasting his philanthropy and leadership with that of the modern-day villains of Enron and World Com.

A big part of the article described Steelman's rise to the top, recounting his first job as a news agency laborer. While working his way through college as an auto mechanic, a customer had taken an interest in him. Turned out he was a banker and Steelman's introduction to the financial services industry was made. Steelman changed his major to economics and from then on everything fell into place. The article ended with the sentence, "It's nice to have powerful business leaders like Nick Steelman, and all those who are contributing to helping Chicagoland's homeless, who are willing and able to do the right things."

Dan sank as he laid the newspaper on his desk. He hadn't given Steelman a second thought in months. But here it was – the spoiler – that one thing that comes along to take the air out of your balloon. He would have liked to bask in the glow of the Taylor victory a little longer before the thought of Steelman contaminated his mood.

Luckily, the rest of Dan's day was packed with activity, taking his mind off the Steelman article. He worked a little later than usual and by the time he made it to his car, the parking garage was close to empty. Just as Dan opened his car door, he heard music – The Eagles' "Already Gone" – getting louder. He turned just in time to see Stanley in his Jaguar, top down, music blasting, rolling up behind Dan's car.

"How 'bout that drink?" asked Stanley, turning down his too-expensive-to-think-about-it custom sound system. Dan smiled.

"Sounds good," said Dan as he hopped into Stanley's car.

They squealed out of the garage, caught a few green lights, and in a minute, were 20 miles an hour over the speed limit on the Outer Drive headed north. Stanley rolled up the windows and bumped the heat on, which made the top-down ride quiet and cozy. Riding with Stanley was like playing a video game without having control over the racing action.

"I don't pass everyone, just those in front of me," laughed Stanley.

Three more Eagles tunes later, the race was over. Dan and Stanley settled in at Burwood Tap in Lincoln Park; with a B&B on the rocks for Dan, a root beer for Stanley.

"I guess you saw the story about Steelman," said Dan.

"Yeah, I did. His PR team did a nice job landing that coverage. His top communication person used to work for me. She's the best around."

"Hey, whose side are you on?" asked Dan as he grabbed a handful of popcorn on the table.

"Yours, of course, but you've got to admit, you wish that story was about you, don't you?"

Leave it to Stanley not to sugarcoat a thing, thought Dan.

"By the way, who is telling your story?" asked Stanley in a tone sounding like he already knew the answer.

"Our PR department is pretty good," defended Dan. "They got us a nice article on the job-sharing initiative we launched last quarter."

"That's not what I mean," said Stanley. "That piece was a feature on your company. It was an article, not a story."

"Article, story, what's the difference? We got in the news. That's what counts," said Dan.

"The difference is that the reader got to know who Steelman is. The reader didn't in your article. It was your company's story, not your story," said Stanley. "I'm talking about who's telling your personal story?"

"Nobody," Dan replied. "I didn't think it was important."

"It's very important. Here, take notes on this," winked Stanley, as he slid a few napkins to Dan.

Stanley grabbed some popcorn and talked between bites.

"One of the most important leadership communications tools, my friend, is storytelling. I've yet to see any leadership program at any major business school teach it. Stories are at the heart of helping your listeners feel your words. They are a great way to illustrate your ideas. Stories help you tell people what to do without making them angry. Stories make it easy for your ideas to break through."

Stanley continued. "Remember the telephone conversation we had just before you pitched the Taylor group? Well, one of the things I said was to decide what you want your listeners to know and what you want them to feel. What you want them to know, I call the *teach* piece; what you want them feel, I call the *lead* piece. Be clear before you deliver any critical leader communications that you know your teach and lead pieces. Well, at the heart of the lead piece is storytelling. Other story-like devices are metaphors, similes, and colorful comparisons, which are emotional and visual in nature. Emotional and visual, that's the key to making it easy for people to remember your words. Leaders who don't make it easy for people to remember their words end up with skinny kids."

As Stanley spoke, it occurred to Dan that Stanley did exactly this. His language was emotional, visual and unforgettable.

"If you're not telling great stories, chances are you're not breaking through to your people at the gut level, and they won't feel compelled to stay committed to your vision."

"So how do I tell stories?" asked Dan.

"Before we talk about how to tell stories, let's talk about why to tell them just a little more," replied Stanley as he ordered more popcorn. "Typical speakers present their content as if it were separate from themselves. The best leader speakers present themselves along with their content."

Stanley took Dan's napkin notepad and drew two simple diagrams.

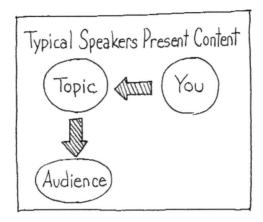

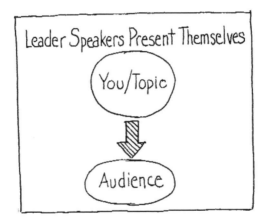

"The people you lead need to know who they're following," said Stanley. "Leadership is a personal experience. It's personal for the follower because the decision they made to sign on with you impacts everything in their life. Make that decision an easy one for them by letting them know, respect and like who's at the helm. Leadership is personal for you because it is impossible to lead – making it easy for people to succeed and feel better about themselves – without revealing who you are. This is where storytelling comes in. It enables you to reveal who you are while embroidering yourself into your content. Storytelling is a huge part of disclosure and connection, which is at the foundation of the leader's pyramid."

Stanley's words reminded Dan of an incident that happened to him years earlier. Dan said, "I remember attending a sales training session years ago. Our instructor was a guy named Leonard. I never really liked him. In previous experiences, he had an answer for everything and was good at making people wrong. He came across as too slick and shallow. Behind his back, he was known as 'Glitter Guy.' That day, I walked into the session with a negative attitude about him. His content was good, as I expected, but what I didn't expect was that he told a story about his daughter. Turns out his wife had died from breast cancer and he was left with raising his daughter as a single parent. He told the story about changing his life to accommodate his new role as a sole parent. It made me think about what I would do if my wife died. I came away from that session learning more about Leonard, and what I learned, I liked. If he hadn't told that story, I'm sure my opinion of him wouldn't have changed."

Stanley said, "Good insight. Stories are a great container for just about any message you want people to feel and remember. There are three categories of stories you need. Think of them as silver bullets in your holster, ready to shoot at a moment's notice. The first category is stories about happy clients. The second category is stories about the great people you work with, and the last category is *your* story."

"So, how do I tell these stories?" asked Dan.

"Stories have a simple structure," said Stanley. "They set the stage and allow the listener to know who the characters are, and where and when the story takes place. I call this the 'Normal World.' Then something happens to the characters changing things irreversibly. This is called the 'Crisis.' The Crisis changes things in the Normal World forever, which leads the character into the third phase called the 'New World.' I learned this from Donald Davis, who is a retired Methodist minister and storyteller."

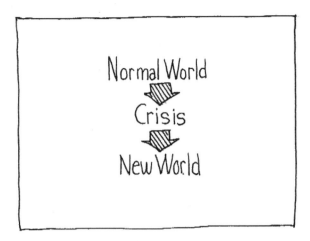

"For example, let's take your old sales trainer Leonard's story about his wife and daughter," Stanley continued. "His 'normal world' story was that he was very career centered, climbing the corporate ladder, and doing all he could to make a decent buck. His wife and daughter are part of his life, but are playing backstage roles. Then the 'crisis' strikes. His wife's death creates irreversible changes in his life. His 'new world' is filled with the challenges of creating harmony between his responsibilities as a parent and his work. If the story ended here, it would be a nice story, but without any significant leadership value.

"Now, to give this story leadership value, that is to advance your listeners toward your business objective, it needs two things: First, there needs to be a lesson attached to the story. What did Leonard learn? Next, the lesson needs to be folded into the context of what he's teaching."

"How do you do that?" asked Dan.

"Ah, yes, one of my favorite conversations. This calls for a real drink. How was that B&B? I'll get two more," said Stanley as he headed to the bar.

Chapter Seventeen
StorySelling®

Dan watched Stanley move easily through the crowded bar. In a heartbeat, he had the bartender's attention. Stanley started talking with two guys wearing Illinois State sweatshirts. Soon, they were all laughing. Dan thought, *Stanley strikes again.*

Stanley returned with the drinks. "As I was saying, to give a story leadership value it needs two things. First, there needs to be a lesson attached to the story. Next, it needs to be transferred to the listener. When you transfer the lesson to your listeners with the motive of influencing them to take action, the process is called StorySelling®. *Storytelling* is nice for campfires and bars; *StorySelling* is for leaders."

Stanley took Dan's diagram and completed it for him.

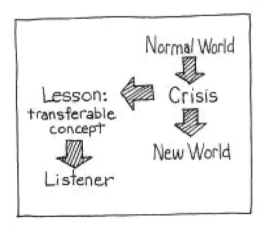

Stanley said, "The lesson Leonard learned and transferred to the listener is called the 'transferable concept.' The real punch within StorySelling is the transferable concept.

"Without it, the story is just about Leonard. With it, the story is about the listener, and in context to what Leonard is teaching. For example, as Leonard describes his 'new world' of juggling activities in his new parental role, he may offer a lesson he learned, then transfer that lesson to his listeners, linking it to his teaching points, so the end of his story might sound like this:

"Since I've been raising my daughter on my own, I've learned I can't do it alone. I've had to rely on daycare professionals, friends and relatives, school system services, and a host of counselors. I've learned that using other people's skills helps me reach a much grander outcome than if I attempt to do it on my own."

"This experience has changed me forever. It's opened up my vision of what is possible. Now when I work with my daughter to set goals, I tell her to imagine them so big there's no way she can do it on her own."

"How about you? Can you imagine sales goals so big there's no way you can do them on your own? Today, we've going to talk about how to work with the people around you to reach sales goals you might not give yourself permission to imagine."

Stanley added, "In this example the transferable concept is the phrase *'There's no way you can do them on your own.'*"

"That's amazing," said Dan. "I could have thought about that story for hours and wouldn't have come up with a link that good. How did you do that so fast?"

"I learned to think in terms of transferable concepts," said Stanley. "I usually can tell another person's story better than they can because I think about transferable concepts in a structured way. Here's how I discover transferable concepts linking the story to the listener:

"I start with the story elements. In Leonard's story, the elements I heard are these," said Stanley as he listed the following:

Story Elements	Topic Elements
sales trainer	
glitter guy	
makes people wrong	
wife died	
cancer	
daughter single parent	
changed his life	

"Next, I list the topic elements. These are the key points I'll make in my talk. I don't know what Leonard's topic elements were, but I guess they were along the same lines of these," said Stanley.

Story Elements	Topic Elements
sales trainer	product knowledge
glitter guy	needs assessment
makes people wrong	Goals
wife died	open-ended questions
cancer	listening skills
daughter single parent	prospecting
changed his life	closing skills

"After I have the story and topic elements listed, I look for story elements that have the greatest emotional and/or visual components. In this example, I've underlined the greatest emotion and visual components in these words:

Story Elements	Topic Elements
sales trainer	product knowledge
glitter guy	needs assessment
makes people wrong	Goals
wife died	open-ended questions
cancer	listening skills
daughter single parent	prospecting
changed his life	closing skills

"Now, the next part takes some imagination," said Stanley. "I look at the underlined words and ask myself how those words in the story elements relate to the topic elements. Somehow the phrase 'changed his life' and the topic elements of 'goals' seem to fit together; goals can change your life. Once I have a good match, then I go back into the story and strengthen the storyline relating to my topic.

Story Elements	Topic Elements
sales trainer	product knowledge
glitter guy	needs assessment
makes people wrong	Goals
wife died	open-ended questions
cancer	listening skills
daughter single parent	prospecting
changed his life	closing skills

"When I tell the story, I make sure I finish with the element that relates to my topic, the transferable concept. The transferable concept here is the phrase 'There's no way you can do them on your own.' As I begin the discussion, I start with the transferable concept, linking my story to my topic. That way everyone gets why I told the story. That's called StorySelling. The story must relate to the topic via the transferable concept. If there is no transferable concept, then there's no reason to tell the story."

"All right," said Dan. "I think I get it. You said there are three stories to tell: stories about wonderful clients, stories about the great people who work with me, and stories about me. Why these three?"

Stanley said, "Leadership stories don't need fancy plots, but they do need great characters. Your clients, your team, and you are usually the best characters. Stories you tell in your leadership role should be more people-centered and less plot-centered. Stories should reveal more about how the characters feel and less about what happened to them. Remember, the payoff in the story resides in the transferable concept, not the plot. Leonard's story plot is about him, but his transferable concept is about his students. Get good at creating transferable concepts that your clients and team can relate to. When you tell a story about you, your transferable concept is always directed at the people you're leading and influencing."

"Give me an example of telling a story about yourself and relating it to your clients," Dan said.

"That's easy," said Stanley. "Let's say I'm speaking at the annual holiday party I hosted for years for our top clients and my key team members."

"Good example," replied Dan. "We've continued that tradition since you left. That party is a smash every year. Clients love it, but I always struggle with what to say."

Stanley said, "It's a holiday party, so it makes sense to have a holiday theme to your story. The guests have arrived, drinks and finger food are everywhere. Soon spoons are being tapped on the sides of champagne glasses, and I walk to the microphone at the head table. I welcome my guests and team, thank them for the past year's great experiences, poke a little fun at one of our best clients, and then I begin the story.

"The holidays always remind me of Christmas Eve parties at my Auntie Sophie's place in Cicero. I remember being a little boy and walking up the front stairs to her house. It was tall, three stories. We'd stomp our feet to get the snow off our boots and hang our coats up on hooks in the foyer. We'd walk up another set of inside stairs to her house. The staircase smelled of pine needles and cigars. As we got to the top of the stairs, I'd hear my cousin Elmer playing Christmas carols on the piano and my uncle Keekie's whiskey laugh. All us kids got gifts from our aunts and uncles – cool stuff like model airplanes, and dumb stuff like socks and underwear.

"As we grew older, our trips to Auntie Sophie's grew less frequent, and soon, we were starting college, going our separate ways, and starting families of our own.

"But I'll tell you, even though it was decades ago, it seems like yesterday my family and I were stomping snow off our boots in front of Auntie Sophie's house, where we were always welcomed and loved.

"This evening, as you were stomping the snow off your boots and joined our annual holiday celebration, I want you to know you are always welcomed and loved in our house.

"Merry Christmas and happy holidays to all of you."

"Wow," said Dan. "You made that sound easy."

"It is when you work from a structure," replied Stanley. "All I did was tell a simple story about a holiday event in my past. That's the part I call the 'normal world.' It's how the story starts. The 'crisis,' the event caus-ing irreversible change, is when all the kids grew up and moved away. Crisis does not necessarily mean a negative event. A crisis can be a good thing like going to college, getting married, or in my case, getting a divorce from my second wife. The 'new world' is in the present moment as I greet the guests. The lesson is my fond memories of Auntie Sophie's Christmas parties, and the transferable concept is the phrase 'welcomed and loved.' This story takes less than 30 seconds to tell, but I guarantee you, as they go back in their own childhood memories and think about great holidays with their families, every person in the room feels my words."

"You're right," said Dan. "As you were telling it, I started thinking about seeing Santa for the first time."

"A big key to making StorySelling work in a leadership role is to keep the story short. A story that goes longer than a minute had better be a killer story. Remember, the longer the story, the bigger the payoff needs to be for the audience. How many times have you listened to a speaker go on and on? I know as I listen to someone go long on a story I'm saying to myself, *This better be good.* If the payoff isn't wonderful, the speaker loses my attention and respect. A good way to think about stories is to picture the old guy at the state fair, perched on a stool, wearing a beret, with an easel and a handful of dry markers, and for five bucks, he'll draw your caricature. A caricature, a few distinct strokes, and a good artist can capture and intensify your features. Your mind fills in the details.

"Great stories are oral caricature: with few visual and emotional words to paint the picture, the listener's mind fills in the details."

"How do you know what stories will work?" asked Dan.

"It's easy," said Stanley. "Anything that evokes a strong emotional response from you probably will have a similar affect on your listeners. Whether you're talking to CEOs or admin staff, we're all remarkably similar when you strip away our roles. Just think of events that move you and be confident that they will move others. Then look for links between those events and your topic."

"It seems the transferable concept is the key to making it all work," said Dan.

"It is," said Stanley. "The transferable concept is the best communication tool in leadership. It does so many things at one time. First, it earns the attention of the listener. It creates that peak of interest that draws listener's attention to the content point you want them to remember.

"Next, the transferable concept and the associated story offer disclosure, revealing a little of who you are beyond your primary role. It's that keyhole that gives your listeners a chance to really see you, and then see a little bit of themselves. When people see a little of themselves in you, it becomes easier to get committed to your vision.

"The transferable concept along with the story create a visual dimension to your language. People will picture what you're saying. Could you see it when I said, 'We'd stomp our feet to get the snow off our boots … '? When you use visual language, listeners will remember it better. Visual language is also the basis for humor and any other emotion you want people to feel. Breaking through is less of an auditory experience and more a visual one. A well-told story is almost all visual in nature.

"And, finally," Stanley said, "your use of the transferable concept can begin to build your personal brand. You'll become known not only for what you know, but also for who you are. Stories package our wisdom in a way that's easy for people to follow. The stories you tell will make the difference in the leader you become."

Dan made a note about the transferable concept in his journal.

Transferable Concept

Earns attention

Disclosure

Visual language and humor

Branding

Stanley continued, "The bottom line with stories and their transferable concepts is they lift people up to see further into themselves and into their future. So much of the energy we need to propel our day-to-day activity comes from what we imagine our future to be. A clearly visualized and desirable future is what bonds the best talent to your organization. Stories make the future visible. The best talent pursues the brightest future."

With that, Stanley grabbed a mouthful of popcorn, lifted his drink, and he and Dan clicked glasses and toasted. "Here's to you, my boy. May your stories stir the hearts of many and make the cash register ring!"

The two men finished their drinks, hopped in Stanley's Jag, and wheeled their way back to Dan's office. As Stanley dropped Dan off, he smiled and said, "Don't worry about the Steelman article. Before the fat lady sings, plenty of people will know your story. They always tell stories about the great ones."

Chapter Eighteen
The Spectrum of Appeal™

If anything about Chicago could make Dan leave, it would be the winters. The year's first snow had arrived the Friday after Thanksgiving, and by early December, the ice was thick on the lakefront. This morning, as Dan and Julie looked over the day's schedule, the temperature was minus eight with a wind chill factor of minus 15. The good news was everything was looking up for Dan and Granite Financial Services. Right on the heels of the Taylor account, two more big clients climbed aboard, ensuring great year-end numbers and fat bonuses. Dan's confidence was at an all-time high. It was not only the numbers, his work with Stanley taught him how to break through and keep the vision clear and his team surging forward.

"I miss Stanley," said Dan, while he and Julie were finishing up. "You know, it's been about a month since I've heard from him. It's like he just disappeared."

"I know," said Julie. "I've called him and left messages. My sense is when he's back in town, he'll show up."

"So he's out of town?" asked Dan.

Julie wanted to kick herself for letting the "out of town" comment slip out. She had a good idea where Stanley was, and she knew Stanley liked to keep his privacy.

"Oh, I'm just guessing. I'm sure he'll be in touch soon," said Julie. Telling white lies, she thought, although not the best policy can be the right thing to do at times. She changed the subject by reminding Dan of the telephone appointments he had that morning, and left his office.

The morning passed quickly as blizzard conditions stormed in and Dan's afternoon appointments were canceled. He noticed several team members leaving early, a reaction to rumors a record snowfall was on its way. Chicago's rush hour combined with record snowfall made for great drama. It was three o'clock, and Dan's afternoon was a bust. Half his team members were gone, and the rest were wringing their hands. Soon they were gone, too.

Dan's cell phone rang. It was Julie.

"Hey, Dan, it's Julie. You better get out of there. I'm bumper to bumper on the Kennedy Expressway and it's getting ugly."

"You're right," he answered. "I could use the afternoon off."

Dan sat at his desk and looked out the window. It was a complete whiteout. Despite the weather, he felt good. Really good. With everyone gone it was quiet and easy to think. A rare moment in his life. The strong year-end numbers made him feel successful again, he remembered it was not so long ago, he had felt he was losing it. He hated feeling like that. Little by little, he had gotten it back. He laughed to himself as he thought about a *Peanuts* cartoon where Snoopy was lying on his back on top of his doghouse, with a thought bubble rising up from his head, asking, "*Why don't people ask 'Why me?' when things go right?*"

Why me, he thought. A lot was due to Stanley. Learning to break through had changed so many things. The thing it changed most, though, was him. Connecting with people, moving with confidence, adding energy to his words, and telling compelling stories forced him to come from a different place relative to leading people. At first it seemed like acting, after a while it was more natural. Now, he couldn't imagine leading any other way. He recalled something Stanley told him months ago, the best reason to break through was who you have to become to do it. Dan was enjoying who he was becoming.

Dan grabbed his coat and headed out. As he turned into the hall, there stood the person he least expected to see, leaning on the receptionist's desk – Stanley!

Dan smiled and said, "Well, look what the storm blew in. Great to see you, Stanley."

"Good to see you, too, Dan," said Stanley as he gave Dan a big hug.

"It's been a while since you've been up here, hasn't it?" asked Dan.

"It's been 15 years," said Stanley. "The place looks good. I like what you've done with the lighting and the new floors."

Stanley walked toward his old office, which was now Dan's. Stanley wore a full-length, double-breasted, black wool overcoat with a mink collar and knee-high Eskimo boots, perfect for Chicago's winters. He tossed his coat on a table, and he and Dan walked together.

"Looks like you've lost some weight," said Dan.

"I always lose a few pounds right before the holidays. That way, when I put on a few pounds during the season, I'm right back to my fighting weight," laughed Stanley.

They arrived at Dan's office. Stanley entered halfway and looked around without saying a word. He moved to the window, put his palm on the glass and paused. He walked to Dan's desk, picked up a picture of Dan and his family, and smiled. Dan stayed at the doorway and watched his friend silently reminisce. A moment passed. Then another. Finally, Stanley said, "Come on, let's take a walk."

"It's a blizzard outside. I hope we're not going far," said Dan.

"Just far enough to get a taste of the weather. Then we'll catch a cab," replied Stanley as he grabbed his coat and headed toward the elevators. Soon Dan and Stanley were leaning into the razor-sharp wind coming off Lake Michigan and high stepping their way through the snow going east on Wacker Drive. Heads down, hands jammed into pockets, everyone on the street looked like refugees just trying to get away. The two men huddled together and waited for the light to change.

"Inclemency brings out the best in Chicagoans," Stanley shouted over the sounds of sirens. "Who in their right mind would live in this weather if at some level they didn't love it? It makes us stronger and we know it. In fact, Chicagoans breed adversity just to get over it. Think about it – all the things Chicagoans bring on themselves just so they can rise above it – the Chicago Fire, Al Capone, this miserable traffic, the Cubs, the entire south side."

The light changed and the wind blew the snow horizontally. Dan and Stanley hopped off the curb and pushed their way toward Michigan Avenue.

Stanley continued raving about Chicago. "The thing that bothers me most about Chicago's bad weather is that the women cover up so much you can't see them. You've got to admit, the women in Chicago are the best. My first wife was from Chicago, good Midwestern stock. She could drink, laugh and make love all at the same time. My second wife – 'Devil Lady' – was from San Francisco. She's proof that living on a geographical fault makes you crazy."

It never ceased to amaze Dan how Stanley could light up his words. He was like a magician. He could make you see things that weren't there. One block later Stanley said, "I've had enough of this. Let's grab a cab." The two piled in a Yellow Cab and Stanley told the cabbie, "We're going to The Art Institute."

"Why are we going there?" asked Dan.

"'Cause nobody will be there. The best time to appreciate art is when nobody's around to bug you," said Stanley.

Stanley knew that wasn't the answer Dan was looking for, but it worked for now. The cab was headed opposite the rush-hour traffic, so in a few minutes they were jumping out and hiking up the stairs to The Art Institute. Stanley was right, the place was empty. They checked their coats, headed up the grand staircase, and sat on a marble bench. Stanley looked excited.

Dan was just about to ask where Stanley had been for the last month when Stanley said, "You're at a party and this guy starts telling a joke. He says, "Two guys walk into a bar and ... no, wait, it was three guys and one guy says ... I think it was a guy ... or was it a girl? Anyway, he says ... no, wait, it wasn't a guy, it was the bartender. So, he says to this horse ... that's right, I remember it now! It was a horse at a bar and the bartender says, 'Why the long nose?' No, that's not right... he said, 'Why the long face?' I think that's what he said."

Dan laughed.

Stanley continued, "Ever notice how some people can tell a joke and some can't? Ever notice how some people can light up a room when they speak, while others dim it? What separates the men from the boys in leadership is being able break through and influence your listeners. If you study the art of influence, you'll discover everybody agrees influence is a combination of logical and emotional appeal. To be influential means weaving logical and emotional appeal into your communication style. Well, that's easy to say but tough to do. It's like a doctor telling you to lower your cholesterol. It's easy to say, but how do you do it?"

Dan knew Stanley well enough to grab his journal before they left his office. He pulled it out of his jacket, thumbed his pen open, and got ready to take notes.

"I like it when you take notes," smiled Stanley. "Over the years, I've studied the natural influencers. I've listened to many audio recordings of influential speaker leaders – King, Kennedy, Reagan and Clinton. Plus, I've listened to many of the motivational speakers. I tried to discover their influencing process. What is it they do that influences me? The problem was because of the wide variety of topics and dramatically different styles, nothing stood out as a unifying process of influence. Then one day about 20 years ago, I had this moment of clarity as I was coaching one of my planners. I wondered, *What if the sound of my voice was like a distinct bright beam of light, so as I spoke it pointed out like a laser-beam on a rifle?* And like a beam of light, when it hit a prism it would refract into its primary colors. But unlike a beam of natural light with seven primary colors, the beam of language has only two – blue and red. Blue for logical appeal and red for emotional appeal."

Dan said, "All this came to you as a moment of clarity? What were you smoking?"

"I was between wives at the time. Instability for me always breeds creativity. Anyway, to expand on the metaphor, if language is like light, then it can be analyzed by spectroscopy."

Stanley drew an illustration on Dan's notes.

Stanley said, "Here's a simple graph illustrating the blue and red spectrum. Since influence is a combination of logical and emotional appeal, I call this the 'Spectrum of Appeal.'"

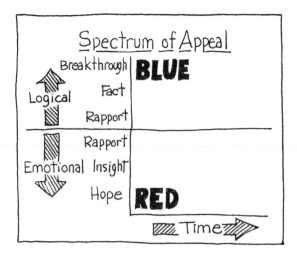

"How do I use this?" asked Dan.

"You'll see in a minute. Let me finish explaining the graph," said Stanley. "The vertical axis represents appeal: logical appeal is above the middle horizontal line, emotional is below. As you move up the logic line, the intensity of the logical appeal increases. As you move down the emotional line, the intensity of the emotional appeal increases. The horizontal line through the midpoint of the illustration separating logical and emotional appeal represents neutral appeal. The horizontal axis at the bottom of the illustration represents sequential time, the time between the beginning and end of your talk."

As Stanley talked, Dan took notes. A few security officers wandered through the rotunda area, glancing at their watches and hoping Dan and Stanley would leave. Dan could tell Stanley was getting into this lesson. Stanley stood and continued. "The first level of logical appeal is rapport. This is when you introduce yourself. Who you are, where you live, what you do, that kind of thing.

"The next higher level of logical appeal includes facts – ideas, data, and information.

"The highest order of logical appeal is *breakthrough*. A breakthrough is an 'a-ha!' experience, which occurs when the listener understands and sees new relationships among the facts, figures, ideas, and other data. Breakthroughs take us beyond the facts. Breakthroughs are the biggest truths, realized when we see ideas strung together like pearls on a necklace. We no longer see the individual pearls, we see their combined beauty. Einstein's famous formula $E=MC^2$ is a breakthrough."

"You're good at providing breakthroughs," said Dan. "Remember our talk about storytelling? Combining the story elements and the content elements definitely was a breakthrough for me."

Stanley said, "It's interesting you say that. Let me ask you this, how did it make you feel when you experienced that breakthrough?"

"Good," said Dan. "I had another tool to use and more confidence."

"What's the second part of my definition of leadership?" asked Stanley.

"The first part is making it easy for people to succeed and the second part is allowing them to feel better about themselves," Dan answered.

"Did you feel better about yourself when you learned how to put a story together?" asked Stanley.

Dan thought about his answer for a moment, then said, "To tell the truth, I don't remember feeling anything about myself at the moment I learned it. I was excited about getting a new tool. A few weeks later, I was preparing a talk and wanted to start with a story and use a transferable concept to get into my content. Well, I banged it right out. It took me less than a minute to figure it out. Now, *that* made me feel good about myself."

Stanley smiled. "What would it be like if you were able to do that for the people you influence? And I'm including everyone you influence – your team, your customers, your family and friends."

"I guess they'd want to be around me more, and they'd be really open to my ideas," said Dan.

"You bet. Would they begin to see your role as a leader in a different light from the traditional leadership role of command and control?" asked Stanley.

"Yes, they would," said Dan. "They'd see me as an asset. They'd see me as someone who made it easy for them to be successful and ... " Dan laughed out loud as he realized what Stanley had led him into "... and help them feel better about themselves." He had just recited what Stanley has been telling him all along about leadership. Another breakthrough.

Stanley looked so pleased. He put his hand on Dan's shoulder and winked. "I think you got it."

Stanley hopped up and said, "Come on, I want to show you something," and he took off up the grand staircase.

.

Chapter Nineteen
Oscillatory Patterns

Dan grabbed his journal and caught up to Stanley in The Galleries of American Art. He was reading the plaque alongside Grant Wood's *American Gothic* – the familiar painting of the dour-faced farmer holding a pitchfork, standing next to his grim-looking spouse.

"Can you imagine spending an evening with these two?" asked Stanley. "I'd end up diving onto the pitchfork!"

Dan laughed.

Stanley said, "Let's get back to the Spectrum of Appeal. Let's talk about the emotional spectrum. The emotional spectrum also has levels of intensity. The first level of emotional appeal is rapport. Emotional rapport is more visual in its language than logical rapport. A short visual story is a great way to build emotional rapport."

Dan asked, "So logical rapport is giving the facts about yourself, and emotional rapport is more like telling a story about yourself?"

"It can be," said Stanley. "Just make sure the story is very short and not too heavy."

Stanley continued. "The next level of emotional appeal is insight. Insights are how we feel about the facts. Typical examples of emotions at this level are surprise, confidence, excitement, humor and frustration. Emotions that are opposites, like happiness and sorrow, are found together in this spectrum."

Dan asked, "In other words, the insight level of emotional appeal is how we feel, both good and bad?"

"Yes, again!" smiled Stanley. "Now, the deepest level of emotional appeal is hope. Hope is the most motivating emotion. The optimistic-hope-filled person thrives emotionally. Your ability to bring hope to your environment is what makes for great leadership, in business and your personal life."

"Let me guess here," said Dan. "I bet one of the best ways to create hope is through storytelling."

"It is. And if you tell a story that creates a sense of hope, how would you transition from the story to your topic?" asked Stanley.

"I'd use a transferable concept and bring hope to my topic," said Dan. "Isn't that what you mean when you say you want people to feel your words?"

"Absolutely yes!" cheered Stanley. "Remember this: to bring emotion to your content, be emotional. Use transferable concepts and the sound of your voice. If you want people to feel your words, *you* must feel them."

Dan loved it when Stanley got excited. When Stanley smiled, his face lit up like a jukebox. Even when Stanley wasn't talking, he was communicating. He communicated with his whole body, his face, his eyes, his smile, his posture, his movement. The more Dan experienced Stanley, the more he appreciated his mentor. It felt good to be around him. Dan smiled thinking, *Of course, that's what leaders do.*

"Now here's how the Spectrum of Appeal works," said Stanley. "Imagine the Spectrum of Appeal graph is like the EKG machine at your doctor's office, that he uses to examine the electrical impulses of your heart. This graph is a long strip that turns on a barrel with an ink pointer positioned with its tip on the center neutral line. Now imagine we connect this 'leader's EKG machine' to a leader, and as he speaks, the ink pointer oscillates between the blue and red spectrum, drawing a solid line indicating when he says something logical – facts and figures – and when he says something emotional – stories, humor, and metaphors. Here's how it would look."

Stanley took Dan's journal and drew a line that oscillated between logical and emotional appeal.

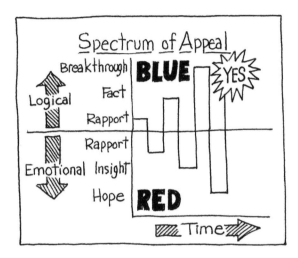

Stanley continued. "This solid line I drew indicates the impact of the language the leader is using. In this example, it begins in the blue spectrum at the level of rapport, and oscillates between blue and red, each time increasing the intensity of the appeal, ending with a call to action indicated by the starburst 'Yes.'"

"So, it's a diagnostic pattern that maps out the sequence and intensity of appeal of the leader's talk," Dan said. "And if you connected your 'leader's EKG machine' to any leader as they speak, we'd get a readout on their talk. It's like the cardiologist who's looking at a real EKG pattern; he can see what's going on in your heart. With a 'leader's EKG machine,' we can see what's going on in the talk."

"You got it," said Stanley. "My intention for creating the Spectrum of Appeal was to illustrate how the best leaders speak. I developed this tool because I was looking for a process to teach leaders how to speak *life* into their leadership messages. After I created the Spectrum of Appeal, which is nothing more than a visual metaphor, I went back to my stack of audio CDs of the best leader speakers and analyzed their work using the Spectrum of Appeal. I immediately discovered the common denominators of what makes leader speakers compelling to listen to."

"What are they?" asked Dan.

"Let me show you," said Stanley as he took Dan's journal and drew in arrows on the Spectrum of Appeal.

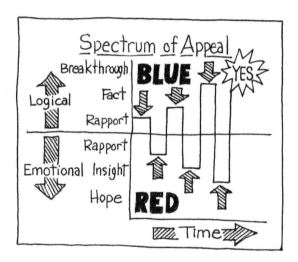

"The common denominator of compelling speech is the oscillatory pattern between logical and emotional appeal, between the red and the blue spectrums. The swings from logical to emotion appeal and back again are what create contrast and peaks of listener attention. When you change spectrums, you earn attention. Contrast creates attention, and attention leads to influence and people taking action."

Dan jumped in. "This goes back to what we talked about months ago about earning attention. Without a listener's attention, we can't influence them."

"Exactly," said Stanley. "Right after I started thinking about the oscillatory pattern in leader-like speaking, I noticed an oscillatory pattern in most things that hold our interest. Nature is full of oscillatory patterns and contrasting elements: the seasons, tides, circadian rhythms, and life cycles.

"We hear it in music. Whether you're listening to B.B. King or the Chicago Symphony, you'll hear the oscillatory patterns and contrasting elements.

"Look around at the Chicago skyline. The architects throughout the history of this city have done a great job in offering harmonious exciting contrasts. Just appreciate the contrast and harmony of the pale old stones of Water Tower Place across the street from the glass and dark steel of the John Hancock Center.

"One of the best examples of contrasts earning interest is where we sit right now. What is great art if it isn't skillfully positioned to contrast elements of color, shape, texture, light and emotion?

"Art, literature, architecture, music and nature all have contrasting oscillatory elements that earn our interest. It's built into our DNA, and we can't help but pay attention. It's as true now as it was thousands of years ago. It's as true in Chicago as it is anywhere on Earth. Doesn't it seem obvious that if you want to earn the interest of your listeners and influence them, your speaking style should coincide with the unifying theme of contrasting oscillatory elements?" Stanley concluded.

Stanley wasn't expecting an answer, so he sat and remained silent as Dan made notes in his journal. A few moments passed. Dan turned a page and continued to make notes.

Then Dan paused, looked at Stanley, smiled, and said, "So, you're saying to break through, I must shift my emphasis from logical to emotional appeal. For example, start with logic, like discussing some revenue figures, then go to the emotional spectrum and tell a story illustrating some issue about revenue. Then, go back to logic again with another principle, then swing into emotion again and use a creative or humorous video to show the principle in action."

"Yes," said Stanley. "Now keep in mind the intensity of your appeal escalates as your talk continues. The logical appeal gets stronger and the emotional appeal gets more compelling."

Stanley drew two diverging arrows on Dan's Spectrum of Appeal graph.

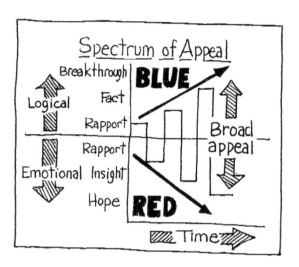

Stanley continued. "The greater this divergence, the broader the total appeal. A key point to understanding broad appeal is this – in the presence of broad appeal, asking the listener for action sounds and feels like the right thing to do. Broad appeal engages listeners. In the absence of broad appeal, asking for action sounds and feels weak. It doesn't move listeners to action. It sounds and feels like you have something to sell. You must know what the strongest logical and emotional appeals are to your listeners, then position them immediately before your call to action. This will result in the broadest appeal at the most critical time in your talk, just before you ask your listener to do or believe something."

"I see," said Dan. "Create a strong sense of logical appeal coupled with an authentic, compelling emotional appeal, and let this energy carry my call to action."

"Yes," said Stanley. "It draws attention to your call to action. It makes it more memorable and puts more energy into it, increasing the likelihood people will align and take action."

Dan put his journal down and said, "Stanley, you seem really convinced this process of oscillating between logical to emotional appeals is the way to go."

Stanley laughed. "You bet I am. Remember, I developed the Spectrum of Appeal over 20 years ago. For 20 years, I've listened to thousands of people speak. Many times while I was taking notes, I'd doodle a Spectrum of Appeal graph and plot their talk as they spoke. The speakers who held my attention and moved me all demonstrated oscillatory patterns. I'd even plot speakers I would hear on television. One of the best examples of oscillatory patterns is the State of the Union address. See for yourself. Go online, download any State of the Union address by any president, and you'll see a distinct, predictable oscillation between logical and emotional appeal. In fact, read the newspaper the day after the State of the Union address, and you'll read how many times the president's speech is interrupted by applause. I plotted the applause points, and they precisely coincide with the swings of appeal."

"Do you think the State of the Union speechwriters use the Spectrum of Appeal when they write the president's speech?" joked Dan.

"Probably not," smiled Stanley, "I guarantee the writers use some template that has stood the test of time and mimics my concept of oscillatory patterns. The speech is too important, and its writers are top people who know that success leaves clues. They're going to stay with what they know works. So should you."

Dan re-opened his journal and made a note to check out the latest State of the Union address.

Stanley pointed to the Spectrum of Appeal graph and said, "Look at the Spectrum of Appeal metaphorically. See the swings between appeals. It's like the swings in an EKG pattern indicating a pulse. The swings are the pulse of the talk, as though the talk has a life of its own.

This is what I mean when I say speak life into your leadership message."

Stanley put his palm over his heart and tapped his chest and sounded out the rhythm of a heartbeat. "Ba-bum, ba-bum, ba-bum."

Dan smiled at his mentor's animation, and realized Stanley had just swung from logical to emotional appeal and in the process re-earned his attention.

"Here's another tip about using the Spectrum of Appeal," said Stanley. "Whenever you're speaking and you sense you're not getting through, switch spectrums. If people are glazing over when you are talking about numbers, switch to metaphors or stories or a snappy illustration. If you're telling a story and you notice people looking at their watches, switch to data or facts or case studies. When what you are doing isn't working, switch spectrums, re-earn attention, and push forward.

"Any questions?" Stanley asked.

Dan said, "Wow, it's a lot to take in all at once. I mean, think about it: unifying themes of oscillatory contrasts, the leader's EKG machine, speaking a pulse into my leadership messages. Where do you get all this from?"

"By paying attention, my boy," said Stanley. "The best surgeons don't get that way by reading textbooks. The best surgeons notice little distinctions with their patients – subtle changes in tissue healing, unusual symptoms, unexpected side effects from medications. Lots of little distinctions over time create the big breakthroughs."

Dan laughed. "You seem to know a lot about surgeons."

"When you're my age, it pays to know the best ones," Stanley joked. "That's what I've done: I've studied the best leader speakers. I've paid attention to them at a level beyond their words. I've noticed little distinctions in them, and, over time, broader patterns emerged in my thinking."

Dan said, "I have to say what you've taught me over the last year has been great. There are times when I feel I have listeners right in the palm of my hand. Your work makes me feel powerful in front of ... "

Before Dan could finish his thought, Stanley interrupted.

"Dan, it is not about you or the palm of your hand, nor is it about you feeling more powerful. It's about your listeners feeling more powerful. You've got to get past yourself when it comes to speaking like a leader. All of this is to make it easy for others to succeed. Their success spells yours, not the other way around."

There it was again, the "It's not about you" speech. Dan never saw it coming. He'd heard it before and it stung again. He thought he had learned this lesson, but apparently not. The look in Dan's eyes made Stanley realize he might have come down a little too hard.

"Dan, I know this lesson is a hard one to get, but it might be the most important. Too many leaders work on changing their followers. I agree, influencing people is a key leadership skill. But on a deeper level, the level I'm recommending, the real work of leadership is growing yourself. When it becomes as important for your listener to succeed as it is for you, you will sound like it, and they will sense it. That's what moves people. That's what breaks through. The deepest motive for great leaders has to be the best interest of the listener. You can't fake this through a slick delivery. People's crap detectors will go off. Dan, I know your heart is in the right place on this issue, but I'm not sure your head is totally there yet. Breaking through to your listeners is not about you."

Dan thought for a moment and said, "You're right. There is a part of me that enjoys the power. Does that make me a bad guy?"

"No, you're not bad," Stanley said, "just not as effective as you could be. Keep the thought that breaking through is not about you on the front burner in your head. Don't struggle with it or analyze it, just keep the thought there. Life has a way of offering moments that reveal what we need to learn. You'll know when the moment is upon you.

"Here's some more advice," Stanley said, smiling. "I've always believed it's never good leadership to talk about important things on an empty stomach. I'm hungry. Let's find something to eat." And with that, Stanley tugged at Dan's sleeve and took off toward the cafeteria.

Chapter Twenty
The Structure of Breaking Through

"I love a good cafeteria," said Stanley as he and Dan walked through the cafeteria line. "I especially like it when there's no one in front of us."

"There's no one in this whole place other than the people who work here," said Dan.

"I know. I love it when a plan works out," twinkled Stanley.

Dan watched Stanley pile his tray full – Waldorf salad, sliced turkey, mashed potatoes and gravy, coconut cream pie – all the while praising the virtues of cafeterias.

"The best cafeterias are in the South," said Stanley. "Southerners live to eat. I've done a lot of business in the Carolinas. Those people love their food. Nothing like a Carolina barbecue sandwich – sticks to your ribs, your arteries – and your butt."

Dan noticed Stanley had a childlike quality to him at times – fresh, lighthearted, engaged in the moment, full of life. As the two men sat and ate, Stanley told stories about the South, all the while delighting Dan with his tales. Watching Stanley was better than watching a movie.

Stanley finished off his coconut cream pie and said, "Take out your journal and let me show you how to use the Spectrum of Appeal as a template for putting a leadership talk together."

Dan pulled out his journal while Stanley bussed their trays. He returned with a damp towel, wiped the table clean, dried it with some napkins, and laughed. "I used to be a busboy in high school. The pay was lousy, but it was a great way to meet girls."

"I bet you did all right in that department," said Dan.

"I did," beamed Stanley. "Girls like funny guys. They also like them thoughtful, too. I have some theories about women, romance, and oscillatory contrasting patterns, but I'll save that discussion for when we have drinks in front of us. For now, let's look at how to put a talk together using the Spectrum of Appeal template."

Stanley continued, "What I'm going to show you will save you a ton of time, and structure your talk in such a way that it has the best chance of breaking through to your listeners."

Stanley took Dan's journal and drew the Spectrum of Appeal and handed it back to him.

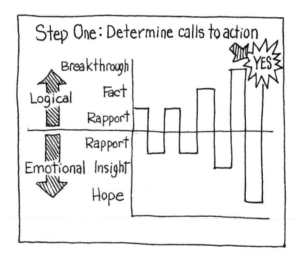

"There are four steps," said Stanley. "Step one: Decide what you want your listeners to do. These are the calls to action and I've indicated them with the starburst containing 'Yes.' There are two types of calls to action, short term and long term. Short-term calls to action are things your listeners can do now during your talk. Typically, short-term calls to action help people listen and facilitate their learning – like asking for a show of hands, having them complete a survey, or participating in a discussion group or a question-and-answer session. You can have many short-term calls to action. Short-term calls to action keep listeners engaged. They earn attention."

"So, if I hand out a spreadsheet and ask people to review and discuss it, you'd call that a short-term call to action?" Dan asked.

"Yes. Anything that gets your listeners doing something during your talk is a short-term call to action," said Stanley. "The long-term call to action is the action you want them to take after they leave your meeting. The long-term call to action generally advances your listeners in the direction of your vision. The listener cannot do the long-term call to action while they are in your meeting. For example, in our current conversation the short-term call to action has you taking notes on the drawing I made. My long-term call to action is for you to use this Spectrum of Appeal template for your next leadership talk. The long-term call to action is positioned at the end of your talk, right after the logical and emotional peaks of appeal. I want people to feel my words when I make my long-term call to action. That's what will help your long-term call to action break through."

As Stanley finished, Dan made notes and Stanley looked out the window at the raging snowstorm. The drifts were getting hip high.

"All right," said Dan as he finished his note taking. "I've got it."

"Good," said Stanley. "Step two: Decide on your points of logic.

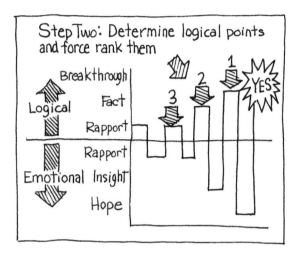

"For this example, I've indicated three. Three points is a good number to stick with. I don't know why it is, but three works – the Three Wise Men, the Three Stooges, three blind mice. Think of three really good reasons why listeners should follow your long-term call to action, then rank the points of logic from strong to strongest from your listeners' point of view. All three points of logic are important. Get really clear about how they stack up in the listeners' minds. Present your points of logic from the least to greatest."

Stanley asked, "Do you remember when I advised you to be clear about what you want people to know and what you want them to feel?"

"Yes, I do," said Dan.

"Here's how we're going to use it," said Stanley. "The points you want them to know are these points of logic. You'll find when you go through this process, you may have some trouble identifying your specific points of logic. That's the purpose of the process. Get concrete and specific about your logic. Too many leaders aren't specific; they mix up and throw in too many ideas and hope something sticks. You must decide what you want to stick. The only way to do that is to isolate the thought and present it with crystal clarity. Leaders must unbundle complex issues and present so listeners can make simpler choices leading to specific actions. That's part of making it easy for people to succeed."

"I bet I know what step three is," said Dan.

"Go ahead, what is it?" asked Stanley.

"Step three is to link emotional appeal to your points of logic," replied Dan.

"Yes, this is the part about what you want people to feel," said Stanley. "Look at your point of logic and ask yourself, 'What do I want my listeners to feel as I speak?' I call these emotional appeal illustrations. Illustrate your logic with emotional appeal. These illustrations could be stories, metaphors, similes, colorful comparisons, music, a snappy video or a picture. I often tell stories for the emotional appeal, and use the transferable concept to link it to the logic. Whatever you use, be sure to use a transferable concept to link it to your point."

"I've gotten better at this," said Dan. "I remember you saying whatever affects me emotionally will probably impact others, too. You were right on. In fact, I'm much more conscious about emotional events in my life and all around me. It seems a lot of life's ups and downs can be used in my talks."

Stanley said, "The great leaders talk about their ups and downs because it reveals a part of them that the listeners can see themselves. When people see part of themselves in you they feel the connection. Listeners feel connected when your leadership becomes personal. What feels personal is what breaks through."

"So, you've found that stories are your best tools for creating emotional appeal?" asked Dan.

Stanley replied, "Yes, but let me be quick to add that it's not so much the plot of the story creating the emotion but the delivery. Your dynamics – your tone of voice, pace, rate – all those things determine how you sound and communicate the emotion. Combine a great story with a great delivery, and I guarantee you'll create a deep spike of emotional appeal."

Stanley continued, "The fourth and last step when using the Spectrum of Appeal when creating a leadership talk is your introduction."

"You see, it's only after you've thought through your calls to action, your points of logic, and your emotional appeals that you understand what your talk is about. Writing your introduction first makes no sense at all."

Stanley took Dan's journal and indicated the position of the introduction and drew a dotted line from the introduction to the long-term call to action.

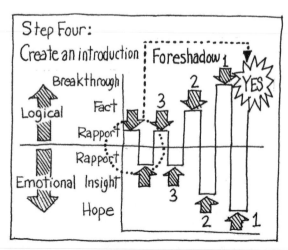

"The introduction should tell the listener what your topic is, why it's important, why it's important now, and foreshadow your long-term call to action. In cases where your listeners don't know your credentials, add what qualifies you to speak on this topic."

Dan said, "I remember this from when you coached me just before the Taylor presentation last summer. You said start with what, why, why now, and hint at the outcome of the talk."

"That's right, and it went pretty well, didn't it?" boasted Stanley, who stood up and turned his chair around to use its back as if it were a lectern. "If I gave you this talk on the Spectrum of Appeal, my introduction may sound something like this: Today, I'm going to talk about how to put together a leadership presentation that organizes your planning process, saves time, and clarifies your key points and calls to action.

"If what you have to say is important, then say it in a compelling way, so listeners can remember it and take action on it.

"You've reached a point in your career where you are in a position to lead. Take full advantage of this time in your life and present your wisdom in the best possible way.

"By the end of this talk, you'll have a four-step process that will enable you to give great leadership presentations."

Dan said, "I get it. The 'what' is the part about creating a leadership talk. The 'why' is about its importance. The 'why now' is that *you* are in a position to lead. Foreshadowing the call to action is 'by the end of this talk...'"

Stanley grinned.

Dan wrote a few notes in his journal, thought for a moment, then wrote a few more. Stanley remained quiet and waited. After a while Stanley asked, "Any questions?"

"No," said Dan. "I think I got it."

"I think you do, too," smiled Stanley.

Stanley glanced out the window at the storm and said, "Let's get out of here or we'll never get home."

Dan and Stanley walked up the stairs and headed back toward the entrance. They walked past huge windows looking out on McKinlock Court, where on a normal day, they'd see the sculptures of the mermen. Today, only the tops of their heads were visible, and by the looks of things, they soon would disappear under the relentless snowstorm. Past McKinlock Court, just before the Rice Building, was an elevator, and above it was a huge painting about 20 feet long. It was a simple painting, white oval clouds on a pale blue sky, by the artist Georgia O'Keefe, titled *Sky Above Clouds IV*.

Stanley looked up at it and said, "I'd guess most people walk right past this painting and never notice it. It's easy to miss because it's not in a gallery, but in this passageway where people are interested in getting to other places. Life is like that. Our life is a passageway, and we're anxious to get to newer and more exciting places. It's easy to miss what we have around us when we're constantly looking ahead."

The two men stood in silence and studied the painting.

"What have you missed in your life, Stanley?" asked Dan.

A thoughtful moment passed. Then Stanley turned from the painting and announced, "What I've missed is the men's room! I'm ready to burst."

Stanley winked at Dan and headed toward the men's room, but just before he pushed the door open, he turned back to Dan and said, "I've forgiven myself for what I've missed. My focus now is on remembering and being grateful for the good things. You've helped me with that, Dan. Our work together this past year dusted off some old, sweet memories.

You've made it easy for me to remember. I feel good about what I've done when I'm with you. That's a very good thing, my boy."

With that the men's room door closed behind Stanley and Dan smiled like a schoolboy. He looked around the passageway. There was nothing he was going to miss about this moment.

Chapter Twenty-One
Christine

Dan was always relieved when the holidays were over. Christmas was too much of a good thing. Too many parties, food he didn't need but ate anyway, token holiday cards from people he'd forgotten about. The best part about this New Year's Eve party was leaving shortly after midnight and being sound asleep by one. Plus business moved in slow motion over the holidays. People were sleepwalking through meetings, with too many distractions and not enough decisions.

Dan took the week off following New Year's Day. He was lying on the couch in his home office watching ESPN highlights of the Bears game when he heard his fax machine spring to life. He rolled on to his feet, shuffled to his desk, and lifted the fax from the tray. It was a handwritten note from Julie:

Happy New Year Dan,

You have some "Stanley business" this afternoon at the Conrad Hilton on Michigan Avenue at 2:30. Lobby bar. It's important.

See you soon,

Julie

"This is odd," thought Dan. "Why a fax and not a call?" Then he remembered Julie was vacationing in the Upper Peninsula in Michigan and probably had no cell phone coverage. He thought, *Do they have fax machines in the Upper Peninsula?* He crawled back on the couch and watched a bit more of the game, but the note about meeting Stanley reminded him of their visit at The Art Institute. After his lesson about the Spectrum of Appeal, Dan noticed the oscillatory pattern of swinging from logical to emotional appeal and back again, or as Stanley would say, from red to blue and back again, in a lot of places. He had checked out President Bush's 2004 State of the Union address, and it was exactly as Stanley described; red to blue, then applause. Dan pulled a few business books he'd read over the last year and the pattern was there, too; *The Invisible Touch, Good to Great, Vital Friends*, and many more. One of the best examples of the Spectrum of Appeal he noticed was in Rick Warren's *The Purpose Driven Life*.

Dan knew the Spectrum of Appeal would transform his speaking. He could feel it working already. But the highlight of The Art Institute experience for Dan was not what he learned, but what he felt; and what he felt was the result of the last thing Stanley told him in the passageway before they left: "You made it easy for me to remember. I feel good about what I've done when I'm with you." Stanley made Dan feel like a leader in a way that he never had. *The passageway experience*, thought Dan. *It's just like Stanley to pick the perfect metaphor.*

An hour later, Dan jumped into his car and drove downtown to the Hilton, where he found a cozy corner table in the lobby bar. He was early. He ordered two Coronas, one for him and one for Stanley. He didn't like beer, but he thought it would be a brotherly thing to do. He settled in and started doing a little people watching when he noticed a woman in a beautifully tailored brown and black full-length leather coat striding into the bar from the lobby.

She stopped at the coat check, put her gloves into her purse, slid out of her coat, smiled, and handed the coat to the attendant. She walked toward Dan, pausing for just a moment to glance in a mirror and run her fingers through the back of her shoulder-length auburn hair. She wore black wool slacks, black suede boots, and a white, silk French cuff blouse with a pearl necklace. As she neared Dan's table she began to smile, a smile that grew warmer the closer she came. She walked toward the table and paused as her eyes met his. *A classic beauty*, thought Dan. *Her look, her poise, her smile. It all works.*

"Hello," said Dan. "Do we know each other?"

"In a way we do," she answered. "I'm Christine, Stanley's daughter."

Dan extended his hand to her and she put both of hers on his and said, "My dad has said many wonderful things about you." Her eyes – deep brown with a dazzling alertness – lit up the room. She pulled out the chair to sit before Dan could do it for her.

"Is this Corona for my dad?" asked Christine.

"It is. Can I get you one?"

"No, thank-you. I'll drink his."

Christine picked up the Corona and held it out to toast. Dan picked up his, they clicked bottles, and she said, "Here's to my dad," and they swigged together.

Dan said, "Your dad is going to be here any minute and I ... " Dan stopped as he saw Christine's eyes pool with tears.

Dan said nothing and waited.

In a few moments she looked up and through her tears said, "My dad won't be here. He passed away yesterday." Her slim shoulders shook as she cried into her hands.

Chapter Twenty-Two
Stanley's Best Talk

Stanley's funeral was two days later. Dan drove from his home on the north side to pick up Julie. The plows had pushed the snow into jagged piles and the diesel exhaust was turning them black. *There's never a good day for a funeral*, thought Dan, *and today is no different.* Today looked like every other day. The traffic, the sirens, the trains. Stanley's death had not changed the world, but it changed Dan's world. He drove with the memories of his friend playing in his head.

He dreaded this and imagined walking into the church and threading his way through the people to the altar and the dark casket. He'd see his dear friend, who just a few days ago was full of life and hopping curbs to beat the lights. Dan knew he would feel the pain. Unavoidable, yet mandatory, visiting his friend and mentor one last time would be a blow to him he wasn't sure he could bear.

Two days ago, his afternoon with Christine revealed much about Stanley's life that Dan had never seen. They talked for about a half an hour, and now during his drive to pick up Julie, he was trying to understand how everything fit together.

Christine told Dan her father knew he was dying. He had been diagnosed two years earlier with a hemangioma. He could have chosen an operation to remove the tumor, but there was a high probability he wouldn't have survived the surgery. His other option was to live with the problem, managing it conservatively with medication, knowing that it ultimately would end his life. Stanley chose to live with it, and every day was a gift to him. He told few people about his health, insisting it remain a complete private issue. Christine said her father believed he literally had to live every day as if it were his last.

Dan learned from Christine that during the last year, Stanley had led an erratic and busy life, including frequent trips to the Mayo Clinic in Minnesota and to a group of surgeons in Europe. This explained Stanley's long absences and unannounced visits. It also explained Stanley's occasional dark moods. Looking back, Dan was beginning to realize the significance of the gift Stanley gave him. Stanley gave Dan his time, time he was running out of.

Today, it seemed time was standing still.

Dan's 45-minute drive to Julie's home was an auto-pilot experience. When he pulled into her driveway, she was ready and walked out to his car. She had flown in from Michigan late the night before, and Dan could see the fatigue and sorrow in her eyes.

"Thanks for getting me," said Julie as they pulled away. "I don't think I could drive right now."

Her voice was weak and her face pale. She looked defeated.

Dan and Julie made small talk about her trip to Michigan. He had so many questions for her about Stanley, but now was not the time to get into the details.

As he drove, Dan remembered Christine sharing with him that Stanley had told just a few friends from his previous business life about his condition, all of whom were unknown to Christine, except for one – Julie. Julie knew. Dan thought back on the many times Julie encouraged him to be with Stanley. Now he wondered, *Whose benefit was she advocating? Had she wanted me to learn from Stanley, or did she know Stanley needed to mentor me to sustain himself?*

Just after merging onto the Kennedy Expressway heading downtown, Dan said, "I'm going to miss Stanley."

"So am I," cried Julie. "During all those years we worked together, he became a best friend to me. Stanley was magic in so many ways. Hollywood could make a movie about him. I remember many years ago one of our planners got married and all of us were invited to the wedding. Near the end of the evening, the band was on a break, and a bunch of people from our office started clinking their glasses calling for Stanley to make a toast at the reception. Stanley was at the bar telling stories. So with his jacket off, he walks to the microphone, completely unprepared for the moment, and gives a toast that brought the house down. The place went wild! They talked about that toast for weeks at the office. Stanley told me later he didn't remember much of, it but he'll never forget the hug and kiss he got from the bride."

Julie laughed through her tears telling the story, and her mood brightened as she talked about the good days with Stanley.

"Do you remember asking me about the best talk I ever heard Stanley give?" asked Julie.

"Yes, and you said you'd tell me after I got a bigger dose of Stanley. Was it that wedding toast?"

"Oh, no," said Julie. "It was something much bigger." Julie wiped her eyes and began, "I was hired as a client coordinator working in the tax department years after Stanley became CEO. I hated the tax department, but really enjoyed working with the clients. At one time I considered going back to school and getting an accounting degree. I talked to human resources to see if there was a work-study program that would allow me to keep my job and go to school part-time. Somehow word got to Stanley, and he interviewed me for his administrative assistant position. The assistant he had was leaving to start her family. I was not impressed with the role of administrative assistant. It seemed like a lateral move, not a step up the ladder. Well, the interview with Stanley changed my mind completely. He promised me if I'd keep him organized and on track, he'd teach me things about business and people I'd never learn in school. He said if I could keep up with him, I'd earn more money than a tax accountant – and have a life."

Julie continued, "Everything Stanley said came true. The first year was nuts, learning about all the lines he had in the water, but it didn't take long for us to really dial in as a team. Soon, I accompanied him to key client and regulatory meetings. I was amazed at the confidence he had in my judgment. Once, he said, 'This business is about people first and money second. Focus on the people and help me understand them. I'll focus on the money and everyone will get rich.' Stanley made me feel important, so I gave him 100 percent effort.

"Then one day Stanley told me his wife, Anna, had been diagnosed with pancreatic cancer. Stanley loved that woman. Anna always showed up at company parties and special events. She'd spend the entire time on Stanley's arm. Anna was beauty and brains, the perfect match for him. Within a month, she died.

"Anna's death crippled Stanley. He took two weeks off and went to Europe with Christine. When Stanley came back, he relied on me much more. Over the next month, he started getting the spring back in his step. He and I were working better and closer than ever."

Julie started to cry. Several times she tried to speak, but she kept breaking down. Finally, she took a deep breath and said, "Within six months, Stanley was stronger. He grew this company with an energy and boldness that jarred the analysts. Stanley said, 'Julie, we are going to put this company so far in first place that nobody will be in second!' And you know what? We did it. That's when we broke the earnings record. That's when we innovated our industry."

Julie paused and looked down, then sobbed.

"And that's when I fell in love with Stanley."

"I was married to Mark, but we didn't have kids yet. Mark was doing fine with his small printing business, and we got along well. Most women would have nothing to complain about, but when I was at work, I felt Stanley's energy and brilliance. I suppose I felt at times what Anna must have felt, and I couldn't help loving that man."

Dan sensed he just heard a secret that had been trapped inside Julie for years. She smiled softly and began again, "The best talk I ever heard Stanley give was in the company break room over a cup of coffee. We were finishing a busy day when we headed for the break room about 7:30 P.M. We worked late a lot back then, and I looked forward to our time together. He poured our coffee and began talking about Anna and his daughter, Christine. He told me he and Anna met in college, got married their junior year, and Anna's pregnancy with Christine was unplanned. He still had a lot of student loan debt and was working two jobs. To top it off, Anna had a tough time physically with the pregnancy and birth. Though Anna and baby Christine were fine, he was struggling hard to make it all work. I suspected this was more than just small talk from Stanley."

Dan smiled as he recalled the many times he had sensed exactly the same thing while listening to Stanley.

Julie said, "I remember the look on Stanley's face when he talked about those days with Anna and baby Christine. He felt he'd missed much of their early family life because of work and money pressures. He told me how he wished he could have been able to bottle up the experience of being a new dad, and so in love with Anna, and bring it forward to today, and just spill it out all over him.

"Then he looked at me, smiled and put his hand on mine. In that instant, I realized he knew what I felt for him. I thought I was good at hiding it. Apparently I wasn't. Stanley didn't say anything at first. He just smiled and waited. I could hardly breathe. Then he said, 'Julie, don't miss your life with Mark. Start filling your bottle now.'

"Stanley continued talking, but I don't remember much. All I remember is knowing that a line had been drawn, and I was alone on my side. I started to cry. Stanley just sat there and held my hand. It was our first and last intimate moment, and I'll never forget it."

Julie sobbed and began to shake. A moment later, she regained control. "A few months later, Stanley left the company," she continued. "We worked well together during those last few months. When Stanley left, I quit to help Mark with his business. Time passed, and I began discovering things about Mark – and myself – that were wonderful. It felt like a new start for us.

It was nice. I remember Mark surprising me with a two-week vacation to the Caribbean. I showed up at his office one day, and there he sat, wearing a wild flowered shirt and a baseball cap. Next thing I know, I was throwing bathing suits and flip-flops into my suitcase, and by that evening, we were drinking rum punch at a beach bar in Cancun. It was on that trip that I became pregnant with our son, Mark Jr."

By now, Dan and Julie had arrived at Holy Name Cathedral where Stanley's funeral Mass was being held. Cars were parked for blocks on both sides of the street. Dan stopped to let Julie out. Before she swung her legs out, she finished her story.

"Two years later, we repeated the trip. This time, with a little planning, I became pregnant with our daughter, Lisa. I stayed at home for the next 10 years raising my kids and loving my husband. The best talk I ever heard Stanley give was over that cup of coffee in the break room. My bottle is full."

Chapter Twenty-Three
Steelman

Dan dropped Julie off at the church, and drove three blocks before he could find a parking spot. As he walked back to the church, he felt relieved. The grieving he and Julie experienced during the ride eased him. Now thoughts of Stanley and their time together comforted him. The lessons about breaking through as a leader speaker were clear. Looking back, Dan realized there were more subtle lessons he hadn't written down. Short sidebar conversations with Stanley now seemed to have even greater significance.

Dan pulled open the heavy doors of Holy Name Cathedral and stepped into the crowded foyer. Ushers helped move people to coat rooms and the sanctuary. Dan signed in on the large leather-bound register and stood to the side in the foyer where a small group still lingered. Quiet organ music accompanied the respectful murmurs of the congregation. The sanctuary was nearly full with hundreds of people, most of whom Dan did not know. As Dan watched people continue to pour into the foyer, signing in and checking their coats, a woman approached him and introduced herself.

"Hello, I'm Amy Easter. I'm a friend of Stanley's."

"Nice to meet you. I'm Dan ... "

"Oh, yes," she replied, "I know who you are. Julie pointed you out."

Dan looked across the foyer and saw Julie. She smiled, turned, and walked into the sanctuary.

Dan asked, "How do you know Julie and Stanley?"

"I worked with Julie years ago when she was Stanley's assistant. I was in the public relations department. Stanley, Julie and I did a lot of projects together. Now I run my own firm in Crystal Lake."

As she spoke and reminisced about her times with Julie and Stanley, Dan noticed her effortlessness with words, her confidence, and her energy. Dan saw Stanley's influence on her.

Dan couldn't help but ask, "Did Stanley ever coach you as a leader speaker?"

She laughed. "Of course! That was Stanley's favorite hobby. Look around you now. You see all these people? I'd bet most of them were Stanley's students at one time. Stanley coached hundreds of people over many years. He never offered, but once you asked and showed him you were ready to make the effort, he'd make time for you. Now that I'm running my own business, his advice has been really valuable. How long did Stanley coach you?"

"For almost a year," said Dan. "I'm curious, what was the best lesson Stanley taught you?"

"StorySelling! Stanley showed me how to tell stories. I use it every day now. How about you?"

Before Dan could answer, organ chimes rang through the sanctuary and people who were standing took their seats.

"We'd better get our seats now," said Amy. "I hope we can talk again soon. It was nice meeting you."

Dan walked into the church. It was full. The only open pews were in the back rows. Walking to the rear, Amy's question lingered: "What was Stanley's greatest lesson for you?" Dan never considered this when Stanley was alive, every lesson seemed great. Now, the question of his greatest lesson started Dan wondering.

He approached the back of the church, glanced to his right, and saw his arch rival, Nick Steelman.

Dan thought, *What the hell is Steelman doing here?*

Steelman smiled, approached Dan, and extended his hand. "It's too bad that it takes an occasion like this to meet you for the first time," Steelman said as the two rivals shook hands.

Steelman looked flinty – stocky as a fireplug, with a coarse, perpetually tanned face, and thick, dark eyebrows. As they shook hands, Dan noticed Steelman's grip was strong and rigid as a trailer hitch.

"Thanks for being here," said Dan.

Steelman laughed. "Why wouldn't I be here? Stanley and I were great friends for over 40 years. He, Anna, my wife and I were close. We vacationed together a few times. I remember Christine as a little girl playing with our kids at our Fort Myers beach house."

Dan noticed listening to Steelman and looking at him were two different experiences. He looked like a linebacker, but his voice was gentle and his manner approachable. As they spoke, the two men drifted down a hallway near the back of the church.

"Stanley and I went to grad school together at Northwestern," Steelman continued. "We competed for everything – grades, billiards and foos ball. We got pretty good at most things we did together. That's what I liked about him. If I didn't play great, I would buy the beer."

"How did you end up at Empire?" asked Dan.

"Recruiters from most of the big firms came to Northwestern to put on a show and discuss their companies. Stanley and I talked about joining the same firm. At the time, he was married and had Christine. I was single. I went with a small company that paid great. Stanley needed better benefits, so he went to Prudential, where there would be less travel, better insurance, that sort of thing."

Steelman continued, "Both of us changed companies a few times over the years and stayed friends. I got married right after I came to Empire. A few years later, Stanley was offered the top spot at Granite and the rest is history. We were always competitors as well as friends."

"I never knew you were friends," said Dan. "Stanley and Julie never mentioned it."

"We kept it under the radar as well as we could. Stanley and I knew where to draw the line between work and play. Some people had a problem with it; we never did," Steelman said.

Dan could see why Steelman and Stanley would be great friends. Steelman was authentic. He was both bulletproof and charming at the same time, and when he spoke, he had Stanley's ability to wrap you up in his energy.

Steelman related more of the history between Stanley and himself to Dan, but paused mid-sentence. Dan could see tears welling up in Steelman's eyes. Steelman reached into his pocket to retrieve a handkerchief, and dabbed his eyes with it.

When he looked back up at Dan he said, "Stanley told me about you. He said you had what it took to be one of the great ones in our business. I could tell that he considered you more than just another one of his students. Stanley taught a lot of people, but he didn't take everyone into his heart. He let you in, Dan. He talked about you as if you were his son. That man loved you."

Both men stood silent. Their grief stole the strength from their voices.

Several moments passed.

Steelman was the first to recover. "I knew Stanley was sick," he said. "He told me a few days after he got the news. I spent some time with him the week before he died. He sensed things were coming to an end, and he talked about you. Stanley thought it was important you knew why he left Granite, and asked me to tell you when the time came. Stanley said I could trust you. What I'm about to tell you goes no further than this hallway."

Steelman's tone meant business.

"All right. It goes no further than here," said Dan.

"Eighteen years ago, my company was sued by a group of investors we represented in a Texas real estate deal. The deal looked good on paper, but I was not in love with the developers. I was hesitant to recommend our clients take the deal. Well, they went ahead with it, and to make a long story short, they lost their shorts, and everyone started suing everybody. We got caught in the crossfire. At first I wasn't worried. We performed due diligence and made all the disclosures. Later, our attorney said we screwed up, and the bottom line was if we settled out of court for what they wanted, it would put us out of business. If we took it to court and lost, we were cooked as well, and possibly would have sanctions against our licenses. What I just told you is on the record as public knowledge. The part very few people know is I went to Stanley for help."

As Steelman spoke, Dan heard the organ surge and the funeral mass begin. Light choir voices sang and thin chimes sounded.

Steelman continued, "I told Stanley everything, which, of course, broke every rule in the book. Our companies were each other's chief competitors. The best business decision Stanley could make would be to do nothing and let the chips fall. Either way, he'd win. Instead, Stanley did the unthinkable. He helped me save my company. Through some Chicago-style financial bullying that only the genius of Stanley could pull off, he made my legal problems go away. We kept everything out of the newspapers and our boardrooms, or so we hoped. Months later, his board got wind of it and Stanley was fired. They let him save face and fed the press some bull about him leaving for personal reasons."

"Stanley liked competing with you. That's why he helped you, isn't it?" asked Dan.

"Yes, that's part of it, but the bigger piece is what Stanley knew to be true about leadership. He let me read the transcript of his argument with his board the day they fired him. I've read it so many times I can tell you almost word-for-word what he said. When they asked why he helped save my company, he said, 'Great companies need great competitors. Like Muhammad Ali needed George Foreman, like Connors needed McEnroe. To be great, leaders need to be challenged. The challenge between Empire and Granite has innovated the financial services industry. We forced each other to be better. As a result, both companies enjoy excellent earnings, and our customers are thriving. To lose Empire in the marketplace would be like losing a worthy opponent who prowls on the other side of the net ready to return our serve with a vengeance and make us stronger in the process.' The board didn't buy it, and asked Stanley to leave.

"Stanley's real love in business was developing leaders," Steelman continued. "He knew strong and smart leadership was good for everyone, especially between competitors. He didn't see company lines. Once he said, 'Company lines are like state lines, when you're flying you can't see them. Looking out the window at 35,000 feet, it all looks like one big country. Business is one big country and its leaders, especially competing leaders, need to keep the whole thing working.' That was the attitude that made Stanley great. That was the attitude that got him fired. That was the attitude I loved."

Steelman wiped his eyes, paused for a moment, then said, "Stanley asked me to help you become a great leader. I'm going to help you do that by competing against you with a fury. It's my gift to Stanley."

Steelman smiled, shook Dan's hand, and walked away.

Chapter Twenty-Four
The Eulogy

Dan took a moment to catch his breath, then took one of the few remaining seats near the back of the church. Steelman was seated to his right one row in front of him. Dan recognized no one else around him. The mass began and the congregation sang. Dan opened the hymnal but didn't join in, his thoughts were scattered as he pondered so many things: Steelman's story about Stanley saving his company, Julie's story about her marriage, his final lessons with Stanley.

The mass progressed to the sermon. By now, more people had squeezed into the church, which was full. They stood along the walls and behind the last pews; hundreds of people were here to say goodbye to Stanley.

The priest celebrating the funeral mass was Father O'Connor; a tall man, in his seventies, with kind eyes. He spoke with a thick Scottish accent about Stanley, his life and his family.

"Stanley lived a complete life," Father O'Connor began. "He was well educated, he loved his wife, Anna, and fathered his wonderful daughter, Christine. He contributed to the world with his grace, his courage, and his generosity. Jesus once said … "

As Father O'Connor continued, Dan's thoughts slipped back to Amy Easter's question that Dan hadn't had time to answer: What was the best advice Stanley had given him? Stanley's greatest lesson – a provocative question.

The greatest lesson, thought Dan as he poured over the list, *Earning attention, leader speaker types, the leader's pyramid? Yes, that's it, the leader's pyramid prioritizing connection, movement, dynamics, and content.*

Dan smiled as he pictured Stanley perched on the bar stool at The Red Head Piano Bar talking about connection and disclosure and drinking Coronas; the time he and Stanley went to the Shubert Theater and Stanley floated over the stage teaching movement; his message about dynamics at Portillo's; and the incredible lesson about moments of clarity while walking back to his office. Precious moments, all of them, and Dan's mind wandered to gather them all.

Father O'Connor finished his sermon and the mass continued through communion. Hymns, chimes and prayers filled the cathedral. Dan's thoughts about Stanley's greatest lesson deepened. *No, Dan continued, The leader's pyramid is not Stanley's greatest lesson. It's one of the best, certainly the one impacting delivery, but ...*

Then Dan remembered StorySelling and felt a surge of certainty.

StorySelling is the greatest lesson, thought Dan. Stanley was full of stories. He almost laughed out loud thinking about the bear climbing a tree he described while pitching the Taylor account. He wouldn't have had the courage to tell it without Stanley.

As Dan replayed his own stories about Stanley, it began to dawn on him that Stanley's greatest lesson was more about who Stanley was, not what he said.

Maybe his greatest lesson was his first, his idea of what leadership is: making it easy for people to succeed and feel better about themselves. Stanley certainly did that for me.

As Dan continued considering Stanley's greatest lesson the mass ended and the congregation rose.

"The Mass has ended. Go in peace," proclaimed Father O'Connor, "But before we leave, Stanley's daughter, Christine, will help us remember Stanley."

The mourners sat down. From the front pew, Christine rose and approached her father's bronze casket. She wore a well-tailored wool jacket, a pencil skirt, and heels – all black. As Christine turned to face the congregation, she took a moment to look out at hundreds before her. The congregation became absolutely silent. Another moment passed.

Christine smiled and began. "My dad loved two things more than anything: his family and his work. I remember the first time my dad took me to work with him. It was wonderful. I was about 8 years old. My mom, dad and I were eating supper, and he and Mom were talking about business. I asked if I could come with him to see where he worked. He looked at me, smiled and said, 'Absolutely, yes, and while you're there you can help me out.' Well, I was thrilled. My dad, the big boss, was going to take me to work with him. I couldn't sleep just thinking about it. The big day came and my mom helped me carefully choose my dress. I remember the new shoes she bought me, they were red and shiny. We took the train to get there, and I remember how grown up I felt in the elevator riding to the top floor. In front of the receptionist's desk was a black sign with big white letters stating, 'Welcome Christine, our special guest of the day.' And within a moment, the area filled with people and everyone was looking at me. My dad waited until everyone was there and said, 'I want you to welcome my wonderful daughter, Christine. She's here today to meet all of you and begin learning about our business.'"

Christine's voice cracked. "And they all applauded and cheered and someone snapped a photo and they made me feel like the luckiest girl in the world."

Christine could no longer struggle against her tears, and as she cried, everyone cried.

After a moment or two, Christine looked up and smiled. She took a deep breath and said, "That happened almost 40 years ago, and today, my dad still makes me feel like I'm the luckiest girl in the world."

Every heart in the room broke at that moment: a daughter's love for her father, never better demonstrated or expressed.

In the first pews, several people got to their feet. A few more stood up, and then, like a flock of birds, the entire congregation rose and filled the cathedral with applause for Stanley, his life and his love.

The emotion of the moment tightened Dan's chest. He felt every word Christine said. It had snuck up on him – he went from just hearing Christine's words to feeling them. He began to become conscious of what was happening – Christine was breaking through. Then it dawned on Dan that Christine had probably captured more of Stanley's lessons than anyone. As Dan listened to Christine, it was like watching for Stanley's lessons to come back to life.

The congregation settled back into their seats. Christine continued, "My father and I walked back to his office. I remember looking out his big window at Lake Michigan and putting my palm on the cool glass. When he saw me do that he said, 'Let me tell you a secret. Every day when I walk into my office, I put my palm on the window just like you did. When I do that, I say a little prayer that God guides me and helps me do the right things today.'"

Dan remembered Stanley walking into his office just a short while back and placing his palm on the window. Dan's chest began to tighten again as the memory of Stanley surged.

"We spent about an hour that morning together," Christine continued. "My dad showed me how his phones worked, where he got his mail, even where his bathroom was. He said he did his best thinking there."

The congregation chuckled.

"He even had a phone installed in there. When I was older, he said many people would be surprised if they knew they made some pretty big deals with a man who was sitting on the can."

The congregation roared, and Dan marveled at the story. He was witnessing Stanley all over again. The irreverence of it all was so like Stanley, and the timing was so needed. Christine had rescued the congregation from its grief by letting them experience Stanley's trademark humor through her. It was perfect.

"My father and I toured the entire office and I met a lot of people that day. I especially remember meeting Julie. My dad saved her for last." Christine glanced at Julie, who was seated near the front pews with her husband, and their two children. They smiled, reliving this special moment.

"After my dad introduced us, Julie, my dad, and I sat and she gave me a present. I unwrapped it. It was a framed Polaroid picture Julie took when we first walked into the office that morning. In it was a snapshot of my dad, me and the welcome sign. Julie said, 'I'm sure you'll want to remember this moment.' That picture has been sitting on my nightstand ever since. It's the best gift I ever received."

Both Julie and Christine now smiled at each other through their tears.

"Time with my dad went fast that morning. Everything was so new and big and a bit overwhelming. As we walked to the elevator and said our goodbyes, I remember my dad holding my hand."

Christine paused.

"Over the years, my dad has held many of your hands, too. When I look out at all of you, I see many familiar faces of people my dad coached as business speakers. My dad said of all the things he did in business he loved mentoring the most. It brought him joy and energy. It brought him life. I want you to know that while he was holding your hand you were also holding his, allowing him to be his best."

Countless heads nodded. Dan noticed many people around him joining in, including Steelman.

Christine, in an elegant and seemingly effortless manner, had captured and held the attention of the congregation like it was a delicate bird in her hand. She was soft, yet confident. Her words were not over-powering, but penetrating. Her stature was subtle, yet her presence was enormous.

Dan remembered a conversation with Stanley in the parking lot fol-lowing his lesson at the Shubert Theater. Dan asked, "You know, Stanley, you seem to really know your stuff. When do I get to hear you speak? I'd like to see you in action."

"The day will come when you'll see everything I know in action," Stanley had replied.

Today was that day. Christine's connection, her movement, her voice, her story, her authenticity – all of it was Stanley. Not a hint of technique was apparent, but to Dan, and everyone Stanley had coached, Christine was giving a master's showcase on being a leader speaker. By breaking through when the situation demanded it, she was honoring her father in the best possible way. Dan knew that through Christine, Stanley's lessons lived on. What he didn't know was he was about to learn his own greatest lesson.

Chapter Twenty-Five
The Greatest Lesson

Christine continued her eulogy, easing into one story, then another in a breezy, effortless manner. Dan felt the room rise with her.

This is magic, thought Dan. *One minute ago this room was grieving. Now they're celebrating.*

Christine's stories continued and people laughed, cried and cheered through it all. She touched everyone in the room.

Then she announced, "I asked a few of you who knew my dad well to say a few words today. And if I didn't ask you, and you've got a juicy story about my dad, we'd love to hear it!"

Immediately, several hands went up. An usher passed around a microphone. Old college friends, neighbors, business buddies spoke, all with memories of Stanley. Their stories were a hit; short, punchy and funny. Altogether, they lasted about 20 minutes. One of the biggest delights was when one of Stanley's more recent girlfriends grabbed the microphone. A slim, tall, dark-haired beauty dressed to the nines stood and told a breathy story bordering on risqué. It was about a getaway weekend she and Stanley enjoyed on the hot beaches of Saint Martin. A few people gasped, but most cheered. She brought the house down when she quoted Stanley, who, after urging they go skinny-dipping, said, "You can only have so much fun with your clothes on."

As good as the stories were, Dan's attention returned to his thoughts about Stanley's greatest lesson. Stanley had said so many things, especially their last day together at The Art Institute.

Then Dan remembered Steelman saying that Stanley told him a week before he died that he thought his time was coming to an end.

It struck Dan like a hammer. "Stanley knew our time at The Art Institute would be our last."

Dan bit back his tears. Several moments passed. Soon, though, his mind wandered to Stanley's impish smile and his perpetual delight. It eased Dan and he smiled inside, remembering their last day together.

Then it occurred to Dan that Stanley would use their last day to deliver his greatest message. All of his lessons were packaged in metaphors and drama: a piano bar, a theater, restaurants, a snowstorm, an art museum. Stanley would not have missed offering his greatest lesson until the end.

As Dan retrieved the fragments of conversation of their last day together, the stories from the congregation ended. Christine rose from her pew and walked to the front of the congregation. The sanctuary grew quiet.

Christine said, "Thank you all for coming here today to say goodbye to my father and your friend. Thank you for your wonderful stories. My dad would have loved them all.

"I was with my dad the afternoon he died. He said to me, 'I feel lucky that I knew I was dying. Most people don't. I've had time to say thoughtful goodbyes to everyone I love. I feel good about that.'"

Christine's voice quivered and her tears revisited her.

In a moment she continued. "As many of you know, my dad spent a lot of his time with many of you, coaching you and helping you grow as leaders. He loved doing that more than anything. After my dad was diagnosed two years ago, his doctors told him to slow down. My dad followed his doctors' advice and stopped coaching right after he learned he was sick."

Christine's words struck Dan.

That's not right, thought Dan. *Stanley was coaching me for months.*

Christine continued. "Then about a year later, he told me he met a man who needed his help. I encouraged dad not to go back to coaching. And then he told me, 'Christine, this time will be my last. This man reminds me so much of me; he's bright, he's strong, and he's so full of it.'"

The congregation laughed. Dan laughed, too, and he felt proud knowing that he had reminded Stanley of himself.

"My dad told me, 'Christine, there are just a few things he needs to learn. Let me do this. I promise, he will be the last one.'

"So during this last year, my dad coached one more time. The morning my dad died, we talked about this man, and my dad said he did well. Then he winked at me and said, 'Make sure he speaks at my funeral just to make sure he's learned all his lessons.'"

The congregation stirred. Many of them knew what was about to happen. Dan's heart started to pound. He, too, knew what was about to happen.

Dan could see Christine connecting with him. She knew exactly where he was sitting.

Christine smiled and said, "I want to honor my dad's request. So if you've got time for one more story, I'd like to hear a few words from the man my dad called his last convert. Dan, we'd love to hear from you."

Dan stood. People turned in their pews and whisked themselves into loud whispers as they searched for Dan. An usher with the microphone spotted him and quick-stepped it to the back of the church.

As Dan watched the usher approach and the sea of people now turned to hear him, visions of that last day at The Art Institute revisited him. He remembered their conversation starting on the grand staircase, where Stanley introduced the Spectrum of Appeal. Again, Dan smiled inside, remembering Stanley and himself sitting on granite benches, drawing in his journal, with the whole Art Institute to themselves.

Was the Spectrum of Appeal his greatest lesson? Dan wondered. *Red and blue contrasting patterns of appeal are a great tool for leader speakers. But is it his greatest lesson?*

The usher finally made it to Dan's pew. He handed the microphone to a woman in the aisle seat, and in bucket-brigade fashion it made it to Dan. By now, the loud whispers had escalated into conversations. When Dan took the microphone, the crowd settled down in clusters like a hundred birds landing on a limb.

Dan looked at Christine in the front of the church. Being many rows back, it was hard to see her well. He instinctively edged toward the aisle to go to the front, but stopped himself, thinking it wasn't his place to take center stage, but several people noticed his movement and they encouraged him together. "Go on, go up front."

Then a few more said it, and then many more, and he looked up at Christine. She smiled and waved at him to come forward. Still, Dan resisted. Then his eyes met Steelman's, one row in front of him. Steelman smiled, then nodded.

Dan nudged his way out of the middle of the pew to the aisle with a bit of nerves accompanying him. He noticed he was thirsty.

As he started his walk to the front, so many memories of Stanley flooded in. He could still see Stanley beaming over his Waldorf salad in the cafeteria on their last day.

Then it struck Dan. A splinter of a memory came to him: the conversation they had by the elevator under the painting in the passageway.

Dan could see it. He thought, *It was* Sky Above Clouds IV.

Once Dan remembered the painting, everything else about that moment rushed in. Stanley suspected that not many people noticed this painting because it was in a passageway where their main interest was in getting to other places.

Dan could hear Stanley say, "Our life is a passageway. It's easy to miss what we have around us when we're constantly looking ahead."

Dan had grown to love Stanley's metaphors, but remembering this one escalated his anxiety. *Was Stanley telling me I was missing something because I was too focused on my future?* Dan thought. *What did I miss?*

Dan's heart felt like it was in his throat. It was getting hard to breathe. He fought back with a deep breath that left him lightheaded and his thoughts swirling. *Don't do this*, thought Dan. *Don't lose it now; not here, not now.*

Halfway to the front of the church, a young boy with a moon pie face and stubby crew cut caught his attention. He was sitting in an aisle pew softly applauding.

Dan thought, *No applause needed; this is not about me.*

It's not about me, the thought exploded in his head. *That's what I missed.*

The impact of this realization stunned him. Dan recoiled from the thought like a stumbling, bleeding boxer. He stopped walking. How many times had he heard it from Stanley? "It's not about you, Dan." And every time he heard it, it cut him. And now the wounds reopened as Dan stood paralyzed just a few yards from Christine and his dear friend's casket. The congregation stirred, sensing Dan's panic.

Anxiety surged through him like poison. The tremors in his hands betrayed his efforts to appear calm. His mind went blank and he stopped breathing. Everyone stopped breathing.

Moments passed.

Then Christine took a few steps toward Dan. She stopped, extended her hand, and smiled.

Another moment passed.

Her smiled melted Dan's frozen moment. He took a deep breath, let it out, and squeezed both hands into fists as he felt his strength and calm return.

Dan took the last few steps to the front of the church and turned toward the congregation. There they were, hundreds of eager people who loved Stanley and each one silently hoping Dan's words would soothe them.

This is not about me, thought Dan. *I get it now. What I'm about to do is for them. It's never been about me. That's what Stanley had been telling me for months. These people need what all people need from their leaders: to break through with the right words at the right time. It's no different here than it is in a boardroom or in any situation where leaders must be heard.*

Dan turned and looked at his mentor's casket. Smiling, he thought, *He's mentoring me from the grave. Only Stanley could pull that off.*

Then, a wonderful memory surfaced of a promise Stanley made on their last day together. "Life has a way of offering moments that reveal what we need to learn."

Dan thought, *This is that moment. This is my breakthrough.* When he turned back to the congregation, he brought this lesson with him ...

Stanley's greatest lesson: *It's not about me.*

Leadership and Breakthrough
Leadership

Leadership - the ability to create an environment where it's easy for people to succeed and feel better about themselves.

Creating an environment where it's easy to succeed

The way you speak helps create the right emotional environment. When you set the right climate through your language, you make it easy for people to be their best.

Making people feel better about themselves

The best experience people can have is a strong positive experience of themselves. Leaders help people feel better about who they are.

Breakthrough

Breaking through is when your listeners understand **and** feel your words.

To influence someone, you need to break through with the right words at the right time. Breaking through means compelling your listeners to take action aligned with your vision.

The test of leadership is action; if there's no action, you didn't lead.

The Leader Speaker
Speaking Styles

Based on two variables-
1. Content Expertise
2. Expressive Range

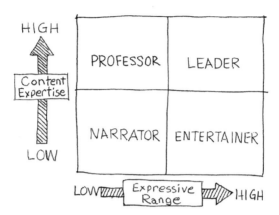

The leaders using each style have a different focus, as well as a central fear they're dealing with when they speak.

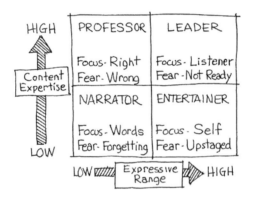

<u>Narrator</u> - Modest expertise relative to content and minimal expressive range. Narrators try to memorize their presentations. They read their speeches word for word. Narrators are so fearful of forgetting something that they become focused on memorization.

<u>Professor</u> - Content expert, but low energy in delivery. Professors focus on being right, overloading their presentations with data and references that support their position. The professor is always adding more content to avoid being wrong.

<u>Entertainer</u> - Minimal content expertise, but an engaging, dynamic delivery. Entertainers focus on themselves, using stories and humor to impact their audiences. The entertainer is afraid of being upstaged.

Leader Speaker - Content expert with a strong, connected delivery. The leader category is the only one in which the focus is on the listener. This creates an environment in which it's easier for listeners to succeed and feel better about themselves. The greatest fear of the leader is that the listener is not ready to grow or act. Part of the role of the leader speaker is to help listeners become ready for growth and action.

To move from the professor toward the leader style...
- Develop expressive range
- Work on and prepare delivery more
- Worry less about the content

The Knowledge Gap

The leader-like way of closing the knowledge gap is to go to the novice's level, then nudge them up to a level of understanding that's needed to act with confidence.

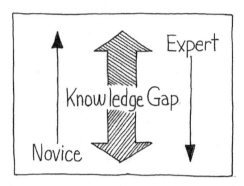

Narrowing the knowledge gap means seeing it through their eyes and understanding what they know.

Go to them first!

Earning Attention
Attention Span Graph

The normal adult attention curve has two points (peaks) where the speaker has their attention naturally – at the beginning and at the end. You can't change this curve. It's built into us.

- Vertical axis = person's attention
- Horizontal axis = time or duration

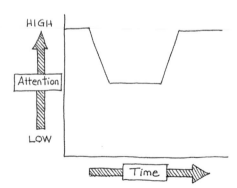

If people aren't paying attention, they won't absorb your message. You won't move them and won't be in a position to lead them.

Earning Attention Cycle
Periodically create peaks of interest to pull the listener in - just before critical points.

1. Get their attention.
2. Deliver the content.
3. Let up a bit. Let them relax.
4. At the next mission-critical point, grab their attention again.

This cycle stimulates listeners, and at the same time, lets them relax and helps them stay connected.

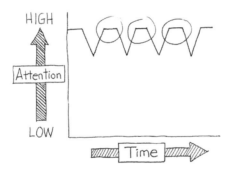

Every time you create peaks of interest and earn listeners' attention, you put them in a position to grow. Leaders put people in positions to grow. That's part of what makes it easier for them to succeed.

Connection
Leader's Pyramid
The Leader's Pyramid represents how the leader speaker can create peaks of listener attention. It's how leaders break through.

Connection
Connection = Relationship
At the base of the pyramid is connection, the most fundamental aspect of creating peaks of attention.

Connection is when listeners feel they're having a personal experience with the speaker. Connection creates a sense that there's a relationship between you and the audience. Connecting creates belonging, a sense of community.

When people feel you're connecting to them personally, their attention naturally peaks, and it's your chance to deliver important content.

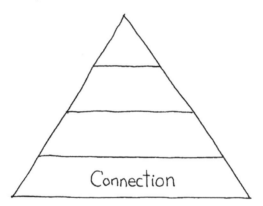

Punctuated Connection
The punctuated connection means alternating connection among listeners to coincide with your sentence structure.

1. Make eye connection with a listener and hold the connection through a complete thought.
2. Hold the connection until a natural punctuation mark (new paragraph, etc.) in your content. End the connection.
3. Connect with someone else, and repeat the process.

Disclosure
Disclosure is when listeners get to know your secondary roles – the person you are outside of your primary work role – husband, father, golfer, Cubs' fan.

Part of being a great leader means revealing the truth about yourself. Let people see a little bit of themselves in you. Let people see you grow. They will identify more with the flaws than the successes.

Stories
One of the best ways to disclose is to use personal stories about growing up. When you appropriately reveal insights into your secondary roles that tap into your audience's secondary roles, you move closer to them. Stories help listeners learn lessons they can apply to their own situations.

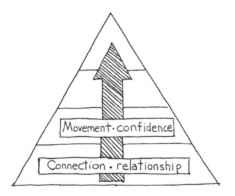

Movement
Movement = Confidence
If your movement signals a lack of confidence or sends a mixed message, listeners may be reluctant to act and/or won't pay attention.

It's easier for people to feel words when there's minimal movement.

Connected movement means holding your connection with an audience member during movement, then stopping and connecting with someone else.

The Stage

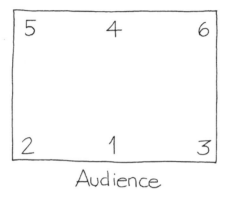

Movement from one position on the stage to another should signal a change in mood or content. When the content changes, it's important to change position. Movement should support, amplify, or foreshadow content.

Position 1 - Used to establish rapport and develop credibility. Used for power and authority. Be here during opening and closing remarks and when delivering strong content.

Positions 2 and 3 - Used for illustrative content like stories and humor. Move to these positions when content is more emotional, conversational, or includes storytelling and humor. Also, use the left and right sides to connect with people who are sitting there.

Position 4 - Used for self-deprecation, irony, or surprise. Retreating to this position takes power away from the speaker.

Positions 5 and 6 - These are the weakest areas of the stage and have the least impact. Used for entrances and exits, and also good for projected graphics and video.

Gestures

Let the energy of the talk drive the gestures. Be conservative with movement and liberal with gestures. Don't try to rehearse gestures.

Dynamics
Dynamics = Energy

Dynamics is the sound of your voice. It's what creates the energy people feel. It includes pitch, tone, volume, rhythm, crescendos, pace, etc.

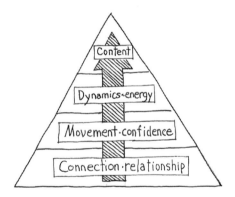

Dynamic contrasts earn attention.

When speaking, contrast an animated delivery with a very calm, peaceful body. Take the main points and dynamically differentiate them from the rest of the presentation.

Just before and after delivering critical content, change the dynamics.

- Pause.
- Get louder or softer.
- Raise or lower the pitch.
- Speak with an accent.
- Use humor; get them to laugh.

The change re-earns listeners' attention and gives you the perfect opportunity to deliver key concepts.

It's the sound of the words — the sound of your voice — that transfers what you're feeling about your content to your listeners. The best leader speakers get people to feel like they do and this helps the listeners to take action.

Pauses

Pauses boost energy and earn attention. Listeners learn and grow during the silences. They make decisions during the silence.

You lead during the silence. You break through during the silence.

Moments of Clarity

Original thoughts that come to you about your topic as you're talking about it. Dynamic delivery facilitates "moments of clarity"

When you allow yourself to express yourself with passion, your energy increases. You feel more alive.

Moments of clarity are facilitated by increased metabolic rate. You become "smarter," more alert, and more aware as you speak. You're able to access thoughts that you can't when you're at a lower level of consciousness.

Authentic Presence

An authentic presence is the ability to earn the listener's attention without diminishing the listener.

Authenticity is key. It's how you gain an audience's trust.

Let people see some of themselves in you so your message becomes more personal. Only when your presence is authentic can your vision become a shared vision.

Content
Content = Expertise

Content gets its impact from the levels of the pyramid beneath it. There's no style in the content. Style comes from the bottom three levels of the pyramid.

Content should be linked to the other components of the Leader's Pyramid. This gives it more impact.

Don't rehearse content; organize it. Rehearse what's below the line, delivery. This is what enables listeners to feel the words.

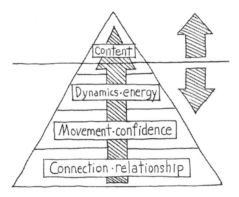

You can't depend on the bulk and logic of content to persuade listeners. People aren't going to take action just because of information. They have to feel something.

Focus on outcomes, not content.

Know vs. Feel

Get clear about what you want people to **know** and what you want them to **feel** <u>before</u> you deliver.

- Know – the **teach** piece (teach with handouts, projected graphics, lecture, etc.)
- Feel – the **lead** piece (lead with delivery – connection, movement, dynamics)

Teach people what you want them to know and lead people with what you want them to feel.

Great leader speakers **alter** their listeners.

StorySelling
Storytelling
At the heart of the lead piece is storytelling. Stories help listeners feel.

By telling a story, you're presenting part of yourself along with the content.

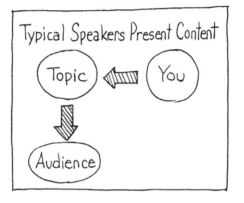

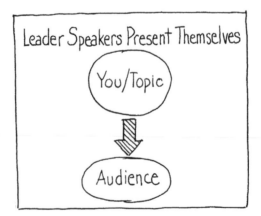

Other story-like devices (emotional and visual)
- Metaphors
- Similes
- Colorful comparisons

Stories
1. Need a lesson attached
2. Need to be transferred to the listener

StorySelling
When you transfer the lesson from a story to listeners with the motive of influencing them to take action, the process is called StorySelling.

Normal World: How the story starts
Crisis: The event that caused an irreversible change
New World: How the world is now following the crisis

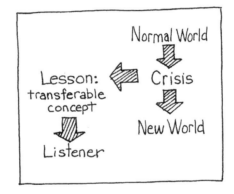

Transferable Concept
A transferable concept, or a word or phrase from a story, can be used to link the content and put the audience in a better position to hear and feel the message.

- Earns attention
- Disclosure
- Visual language and humor
- Branding

The story must relate to the topic via the transferable concept.

Discovering Transferable Concepts
1. List the story elements.
2. List the topic elements (key points).
3. Underline the story elements that have the greatest emotional and/or visual components.
4. Identify how the underlined words in the story elements relate to the topic elements.
5. Go back into the story and strengthen the storyline that relates to the topic.
6. Finish the story with the element that relates to the topic, the transferable concept.

Leonard:

Story Elements	Topic Elements
sales trainer	product knowledge
glitter guy	needs assessment
makes people wrong	Goals
wife died	open-ended questions
cancer	listening skills
daughter single parent	prospecting
changed his life	closing skills

Spectrum of Appeal

To influence a person, you must appeal cognitively (logically) AND emotionally.

The Spectrum of Appeal is a diagnostic pattern that maps out the sequence and intensity of appeal of a leader's talk.

The primary colors of the "beam of language" are blue (logical appeal) and red (emotional).

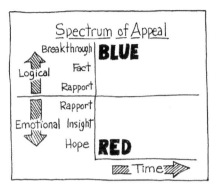

- The vertical axis represents appeal, with logical appeal above the middle horizontal line and emotional appeal below the line.
- The horizontal axis represents sequential time; the time between the beginning and end of the communication.

As you move up the logic line, the intensity of the logical appeal increases, and as you move down the emotional line, the intensity of the emotional appeal increases. The middle horizontal line represents neutral appeal.

Leader speakers begin in the blue spectrum (rapport) and oscillate between blue and red, each time increasing the intensity of the appeal, ending with a call to action.

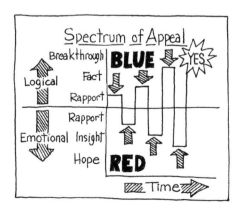

The common denominator of compelling speaking is its oscillatory pattern between logical and emotional appeal, between the red and the blue spectrums. The swings from logical to emotional appeal and back again are what create contrast and peaks of listener attention.

When you change spectrums, you earn attention. Contrast creates attention and attention leads to influence and people taking action.

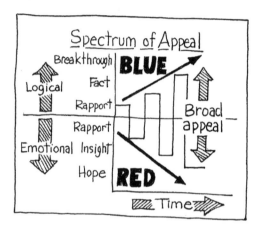

In the presence of broad appeal, asking the listener for action sounds and feels like the right thing to do. Broad appeal engages listeners.

In the absence of broad appeal, asking for action sounds and feels weak. It doesn't move listeners to action. It sounds and feels like you have something to sell.

Influencing people is a key leadership skill, but on a deeper level, the real work of leadership is growing yourself.

When it becomes as important for your listeners to succeed as it is for you, you will sound like it and they will sense it. That's what moves people. That's what breaks through.

Spectrum of Appeal Template

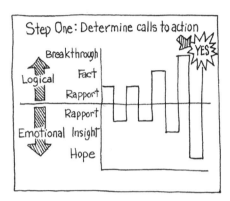

Four Steps to Putting a Leadership Talk Together

1. Decide what you want listeners to do. These are the calls to action.

Short-term calls to action are things that listeners can do during the talk. They help people listen and facilitate learning (i.e., asking for a show of hands, having them complete a survey, participating in a discussion group or a question-and-answer session).

The long-term call to action is the action you want them to take after they leave. It advances listeners in the direction of your vision.

2. Identify and force rank points of logic. List three good reasons listeners should follow your long-term call to action.

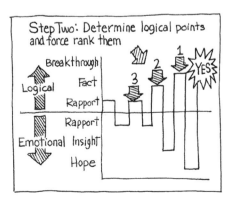

3. Link emotional appeal to the points of logic. Illustrate with stories, metaphors, similes, colorful comparisons, music, etc. Use transferable concepts to link the emotional appeals to the logic.

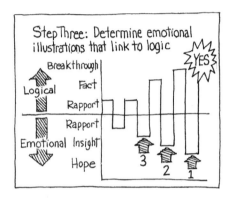

4. Create the introduction
- Tell what you're going to talk about (one- to two-sentence overview).
- Tell why you're going to talk about it, the outcome (the logical reasons).
- Tell them "why now." Usually involves some crisis or opportunity or fear that moves people to take action. The "why now" relates to your listeners.
- Foreshadow call to action. This is the next step, or what you want them to do.

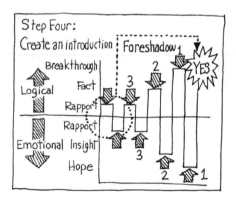

Glossary of Terms

Above the Line / Below the Line – Above the line is content, below the line is delivery, referring to the interface between dynamics and content on the Leader's Pyramid.

Authentic Presence – Your ability to earn and hold attention (creating a peak of attention) resulting in your listeners becoming more aware (conscious/alert) of what they need to know to be successful without diminishing your listeners.

Broad Appeal – The total appeal impact when combining the height of your logical appeal with the depth of your emotional appeal. Creating broad appeal is one of the goals of speaking like a leader. The broadest appeal is created immediately prior to asking for long-term action.

Connected Movement – Holding your connection during movement.

Connection – The experience of the listeners when they feel they have your full attention – relationship.

Cross the Line – The process of transitioning from logical to emotional (emotional to logical) domains. The "line" refers to the neutral appeal line on the Spectrum of Appeal. When crossing that line, changes occur in connection, movement and dynamics.

Disclosure – Revealing your secondary roles that appeal to your listeners' secondary roles.

Dynamic Distinction (contrast) – Surrounding target word or phrase with contrasting dynamics.

Dynamics – How you sound (volume, pitch, tone, tempo, etc.) – energy.

Lead Piece – Content designed to answer the question, "What do you want your listeners to feel now?" Lead with your delivery – connection, movement, dynamics.

Leader's Pyramid – The foundational aspects of a presentation that create and hold attention – connection, movement, dynamics, and content.

Leadership – Leadership is creating an environment where it's easy for people to succeed and feel better about themselves.

Living an Event – Speaking about an event in the present tense as if you were living it now (speaking from the inside, looking out).

Long-Term Call to Action – Asking listeners to do something after your presentation that they cannot do during your presentation (following through on an initiative, such as buying something, losing weight). Long-term calls to action lead to outcomes that help listeners advance their lives.

Most Compelling Emotion – Emotional illustrations (stories, metaphors, comparisons, tone of voice, etc.) that link to your points of logic and lead your listeners to feel your words.

Movement – Movement signals confidence.

Narrating an Event – Speaking about an event in past tense (speaking from the outside, looking in).

Pace – The interval of time (silence) you allow between your thoughts that allows listeners to learn and make decisions. Pace allows you to sustain the relationship (impact) beyond the words.

Performance Anxiety – Normal excitement that accompanies the beginning of a presentation and subsides after a few minutes of speaking.

Power Position – Downstage center.

Primary Role – Your role as the speaker, teacher, facilitator, and/or coach.

Rate – The number of words per minute you speak.

Red/Blue Shift (blue/red shift) – Changing the domain of your appeal from emotional to logical appeal and vice-versa. This change of domain is accompanied by changes in connection, movement and dynamics.

Rehearsing Impact / Rehearsing Below the Line – Rehearsing the connection, movement and dynamics of your presentation (the "line" refers to the interface between dynamics and content on the Leader's Pyramid).

Secondary Role – Your role in the non-work areas of your life; son, daughter, parent, ballroom dancer, gourmet cook, singer, etc.

Short-Term Call to Action – Asking listeners to do something during the presentation that advances learning (answering questions, discussion groups, completing assessments, etc). You may have numerous short-term calls to action during a 30- to 45-minute presentation.

Silent Connection – Making a connection with a listener without speaking.

Spectrum of Appeal – The oscillatory pattern created by moving between the domains of logical and emotional appeal

Stage Fright – Crippling anxiety that makes it impossible for a leader to communicate in front of a group.

StorySelling – A leadership tool that blends the logical appeal of the key points, facts and data with the emotional appeal of stories, colorful comparisons and metaphors. When logic and emotion are blended, each becomes more appealing. StorySelling makes the facts of a presentation more friendly, the stories more relevant, and the speaker more compelling.

Strongest Logic Points – Cognitive reasons for listeners to act on long-term call to action. Logic points (usually presented in groups of three) are presented in the sequence of strong, stronger, and strongest logic.

Teach Piece – Content designed to answer the question, "**What do you want your listeners to know now?**" Teach with handouts, lecture, projected graphics, etc.

Transferable Concept – Using a phrase/concept from your story/illustration and applying it to your content.

True Voice – How you sound (dynamic quality) when you're at your best.

Your Next Steps

If you enjoyed **Break Through – A Leader's Greatest Lesson,** you'll love the additional leadership development-related products and services I offer:

- A *free* Spectrum of Appeal™ four-step leadership presentation template. Download by visiting www.speaklikealeader.com
- **Break Through – A Leader's Greatest Lesson** keynote presentation, ideal for corporate annual meetings and retreats
- **Break Through – A Leader's Greatest Lesson** compact disc audio book read by the author
- **Speak Like a Leader**™ Workshop – a two-day, full-participation workshop that teaches the principles of Break Through
- **Speak Like a Leader**™ one-on one coaching, designed as a follow-up to the two-day workshop
- **Speak Like a Leader**™ train-the-trainer program – licenses the intellectual property of **Break Through – A Leader's Greatest Lesson** to your leadership trainers

Dr. Paul Homoly, CSP
Homoly Communications Institute
2125 Southend Drive • Suite 250 • Charlotte, NC 28203
800-294-9370 • info@paulhomoly.com • www.speaklikealeader.com